ORGANIZING SOLUTIONS FOR ADHD DECODED

MOVE FROM CHAOS TO CALM, BOOST FOCUS, AND FEEL CONFIDENT WITH SIMPLE HACKS TO ORGANIZE AND DECLUTTER YOUR PERSONAL AND PROFESSIONAL LIFE

VISIONARY PRESS

© **Copyright 2024 Lisa Kepple - All rights reserved.**

The content within this book may not be reproduced, duplicated or transmitted without direct written permission from the author or the publisher.

Under no circumstances will any blame or legal responsibility be held against the publisher, or author, for any damages, reparation, or monetary loss due to the information contained within this book. Either directly or indirectly. You are responsible for your own choices, actions, and results.

Legal Notice:

This book is copyright protected. This book is only for personal use. You cannot amend, distribute, sell, use, quote or paraphrase any part, of the content within this book, without the consent of the author or publisher.

Disclaimer Notice:

Please note the information contained within this document is for educational and entertainment purposes only. All effort has been expended to present accurate, up-to-date, and reliable, complete information. No warranties of any kind are declared or implied. Readers acknowledge that the author is not engaging in the rendering of legal, financial, medical or professional advice. The content within this book has been derived from various sources. Please consult a licensed professional before attempting any techniques outlined in this book.

By reading this document, the reader agrees that under no circumstances is the author responsible for any losses, direct or indirect, which are incurred as a result of the use of the information contained within this document, including, but not limited to, — errors, omissions, or inaccuracies.

TABLE OF CONTENTS

Introduction   7

1. UNDERSTANDING ADHD AND ITS INFLUENCE ON ORGANIZATION   11
   Reimagining ADHD: From Liability to Superpower   12
   Executive Dysfunction Decoded   14
   The Science of ADHD and Organization   16
   Embracing Neurodiversity in Everyday Tasks   18

2. MINDSET SHIFTS FOR SUCCESSFUL ORGANIZATION   23
   Turning Challenges into Opportunities   24
   Cultivating a Growth Mindset with ADHD   25
   Empowerment through Self-Discovery   27
   Overcoming Negative Self-Perception   30

3. CREATING A FOUNDATION FOR ORGANIZATION   33
   Building a Routine That Works for You   33
   Personalized Time Management Strategies   37
   Setting Achievable Goals and Objectives   39

4. STRATEGIES FOR DECLUTTERING YOUR SPACE   43
   Quick Wins to Boost Your Confidence   44
   Step-by-Step Decluttering Hacks   46
   Using the Pomodoro Technique for Decluttering   48
   Maintaining a Clutter-Free Zone   50

5. ENHANCING FOCUS AND REDUCING DISTRACTIONS   53
   Creating Focus-Friendly Environments   53
   Using Stimming as a Tool   57
   Tech Tools to Enhance Focus   58
   Managing Time Blindness   60
   Battling ADHD Paralysis   62

6. EMOTIONAL REGULATION AND ITS IMPACT ON
   ORGANIZATION   65
   Understanding Emotional Dysregulation   66
   Strategies for Managing RSD   67
   Mindfulness Techniques for Emotional Control   69
   Cognitive Restructuring for Emotional Balance   71
   Training Yourself in Cognitive Flexibility   73
   Building Resilience in Daily Life   74

7. TASK INITIATION AND COMPLETION
   TECHNIQUES   79
   Overcoming Procrastination   80
   Reward Systems for Motivation   82
   Task Breakdown: From Overwhelm to Action   84
   Maintaining Momentum in Task Completion   86

8. LEVERAGING YOUR ADHD TRAITS FOR
   ENHANCED PRODUCTIVITY   89
   Embracing Hyperfocus as a Strength   89
   Unleashing the Power of Creativity   92
   Hyperactivity as a Superpower   93

9. ROOM-SPECIFIC STRATEGIES FOR TARGETED
   ORGANIZATION   97
   Conquer Your Kitchen!   97
   Creating a Peaceful Bedroom Sanctuary   99
   Home Office Harmony   100
   Living Room Liberation!   101
   Bathroom Breakthrough!   103

10. DEVELOPING STRUCTURED PROGRAMS AND
    ROUTINES   105
    Design Your Own 30-Day Challenge   105
    Daily Routines for Consistency   107
    Accountability Partners   109
    Using Technology to Support Your Routine   111

11. SELF-REFLECTION AND PERSONAL GROWTH   113
    Identifying Your Strengths and Weaknesses   113
    Journaling for ADHD Self-Discovery   115
    Reflection Activities to Foster Growth   117
    Embracing Continuous Improvement   119

12. LONG-TERM SUCCESS AND EMPOWERMENT 121
   Viewing ADHD as a Lifelong Asset 121
   Empowerment through Education and Advocacy 123
   Celebrating Success and Looking Forward 124

   Conclusion 129
   References 131

GET YOUR FREE BONUS EBOOK:

Money Management for ADHD Decoded: A 30-Day Guide to Financial Clarity

Tired of paying ADHD tax? I was too! That's why I'm sharing how I learned to work WITH my brain, not against it. From impulsive spending to forgotten bills - I've got you covered. Think of it as your personalized ADHD tax relief guide. Because your brain shouldn't cost you extra money. Grab yours today!

To get your copy, scan the QR code below:

INTRODUCTION

Every journey toward organization begins with a single truth: you aren't broken, and you never were. Your brain is uniquely wired, and that's where we'll find your strength.

A typical Monday morning for me used to be chaos. The alarm clock would blare like a foghorn. I'd reach over, fumbling to silence it, hitting the snooze button more than once. After knocking over a stack of whatever I'd thrown haphazardly on my nightstand, along with yesterday's coffee cup, I'd leap out of bed. While falling over a pile of clothes on my way to the bathroom, the cursing and self-loathing would ramp up. Already late, the mad scramble to find my keys, shoes, phone, and whatever else I needed to have with me would follow. The day had barely begun, and it already felt like I was losing a game I didn't want to be playing. By the time I left the house, I was stressed, irritable, and perplexed as to why every morning had to start this way.

Perhaps this scenario feels familiar to you. Many adults with ADHD experience a daily whirlwind like this. We have all the best intentions, but maintaining organization and focus often seems impossible. Research shows that adults with ADHD often struggle with executive functioning, which impacts their ability to plan, organize, and manage time. This can lead to chronic disorganization and feelings of overwhelm… something I am very familiar with.

ADHD is something I've lived with my whole life… but, like many people, I wasn't diagnosed until well into adulthood. For me, this was a huge relief. It explained so much about me and allowed me to stop beating myself up about how I felt I was failing. Plus, it gave me something concrete to work with, and I was able to start finding strategies. My goal now is to share some of those strategies with you, and I hope you'll find them to be as much of a game-changer as I did.

My mission is to inspire change and help readers toward personal growth, as I strongly believe that knowledge is the gateway to self-discovery. Since receiving my diagnosis, I know this to be true. Simply getting that confirmation of what I'd already started to suspect told me so much about myself and gave me the tools I needed to move forward. Personal growth is an ongoing journey, and I'm sure I'll never be done, but I'm so much happier (and so much less stressed!) now, and this is something I hope to be able to bring to you, too.

This book is here to offer a new way forward. My goal is to help you transform how you approach organizing and decluttering your life as someone with ADHD. It's not about perfection or fitting into a mold; it's about embracing the way your mind works and turning what may seem like weaknesses into strengths. You have the power to create a space that brings you calm and focus, rather than chaos and stress. How do I know? Because I've done it.

What you'll find here are strategies specifically tailored to the ADHD mind. This guidance will help you increase your focus, reduce your stress, and discover a greater sense of emotional well-being. You'll learn ways to set up your environment to support your goals, making daily tasks more manageable and less daunting —something I've no doubt you feel is long overdue.

The book is organized into clear, actionable sections. Each chapter focuses on a different aspect of organizing and decluttering with ADHD, sometimes focusing on you and your processes and sometimes focusing on your space. We'll start by understanding ADHD behavior and how it affects our organizational skills, moving to implementing quick wins and establishing long-term strategies, and then we'll talk about how you can keep growing and building on what you've accomplished. By the end of the book, you'll have a comprehensive toolkit to draw upon. You might notice that some strategies come up more than once. This is because each strategy can help in multiple ways, and as you apply them, you'll begin to see how versatile they are. You may want to start a dedicated journal or notebook to keep track of your personal reflections and goals as you go—this is what I did, and it made a massive difference to both my organization and my ability to recognize my wins (which weren't always obvious until I wrote them down). Every journey has its challenges, but this is your pathway to a calmer, more organized life, and each roadblock you encounter along the way is something you can learn from.

As you turn the pages, believe that change is possible—and it's within your reach. I can confidently tell you that, despite being someone who once felt buried by clutter, I have found both a sense of peace and my living room floor! This is your journey to a more organized and peaceful life… and it begins right now!

1

UNDERSTANDING ADHD AND ITS INFLUENCE ON ORGANIZATION

Every pile of clutter, every missed deadline, every overwhelming moment has been trying to tell us something important about how our minds work. Today, we start listening.

Have you ever experienced a moment, perhaps in the middle of a hectic day, when you've found yourself staring at a cluttered desk or a chaotic schedule, feeling completely overwhelmed by the disorder that seems to follow you everywhere? You might wonder why tasks that seem straightforward to other people feel like monumental challenges to you. I used to be very hard on myself about this, but as you know yourself, it's not about a lack of effort or desire—it's the unique way your ADHD brain interacts with the world around you. Many adults with ADHD share this experience, grappling with organization and focus in a society that often misunderstands their capabilities. The reality is that ADHD affects how you process information, prioritize tasks, and maintain routines, often leaving you feeling like you're swimming against the tide.

ADHD impacts your organizational skills, not because you lack strategies but because ADHD affects your persistence and consistency in applying them. This doesn't mean you're doomed to live in chaos, though. It means you have the chance to reframe how you see and manage your ADHD traits and turn them into strengths rather than liabilities—and this is something I've found to be very empowering.

REIMAGINING ADHD: FROM LIABILITY TO SUPERPOWER

For too long, society has viewed ADHD through a lens of deficits. We hear about inattention, hyperactivity, and impulsivity as if these symptoms are all there is to the story. But what if we shift the perspective? What if these characteristics are not just challenges but also incredible assets? Many successful people have ADHD and attribute their achievements, in part, to the unique ways their minds work. Figures like Simone Biles and Michael Phelps have excelled, essentially transforming their ADHD into a superpower. Simone Biles has explicitly spoken about how she learned to channel her hyperfocus when she was working through her routines, also leaning into her high energy and using her creative thinking to help her envision new routines that other people had never thought of.

Let's think, for a moment, about the creativity that often accompanies ADHD. It's become a cliché to say that people with ADHD think outside the box, but like most clichés, this is actually a reality backed both by research and by the stories of countless artists, entrepreneurs, and thinkers who have used their ADHD as a springboard for groundbreaking ideas. Creativity isn't always about art or inventions; it can also be about everyday solutions— and finding new ways to organize your space or manage your time is one of them. Your ability to see things differently is a gift, and it's one that can lead to unique solutions and approaches that others might overlook.

Another trait often seen in ADHD is boundless energy. This often feels overwhelming for me, especially when it seems to scatter my focus, but it can be channeled into productivity. With the right strategies, your energy can drive you to complete tasks with a speed and intensity that surprises even you. The secret is to direct that energy toward tasks that align with your interests and goals—and we'll look at how you can do that shortly.

Then, there's the hyperfocus that Simone Biles has found so helpful: the ability to become so engrossed in an activity that everything else fades away. While there's a risk that it can sometimes lead you to neglect other responsibilities, hyperfocus can also be an incredible asset when harnessed effectively. It gives you the ability to dive deep into a project and lose yourself in the flow of work, which can lead to exceptional results. This becomes extra helpful when you're able to recognize that you're in hyperfocus. Once you can do this, you can learn to guide it toward productive ends, and this can transform how you approach tasks and projects.

Channeling all of these qualities, for most people, requires a mindset shift. You have to view your ADHD as a collection of potential superpowers rather than as limitations. I know that's a frustrating thing to hear when you've felt misunderstood for most of your life, but for me, choosing to see it this way was very empowering, and it allowed me to redefine my relationship with ADHD. Techniques such as positive self-talk and affirmations are hugely helpful in this transformation, helping you to reinforce the belief that you possess unique strengths, and we'll look more closely at these in the next chapter.

EXECUTIVE DYSFUNCTION DECODED

Your brain is like a computer's operating system, and your executive functions are like the software involved in managing multiple tasks. This system organizes, prioritizes, and directs your activities every day, and it involves your working memory, cognitive flexibility, and self-control. For those of us with ADHD, executive dysfunction is like the computer running too many programs at once, slowing down, and struggling to process inputs efficiently. It impacts everything from remembering appointments to deciding what task to tackle next. I spent a long time thinking that this was a flaw in my character, but since my diagnosis, I've understood it to be the unique way in which my brain processes information, and this has helped me to be more compassionate with myself.

As I have no doubt you're very well aware, executive dysfunction can make even simple tasks feel daunting. It might affect how you manage your time or organize your environment. You may find yourself standing in a cluttered room, not knowing where to start, or sitting in front of a to-do list that seems endless. As we'll discuss moving forward, breaking tasks into smaller, more manageable steps can simplify this. For me, checklists have been a savior. They give me a visual representation of my progress, and this motivates me to keep moving forward.

I used to laugh at myself for putting tiny tasks on my to-do lists, but I've since learned that this is actually something many people recommend. If you break the tasks on your list down into their component parts, you can tackle them one at a time (which is less overwhelming) *and* have the satisfaction of crossing them all off. To give you an example, I needed to send out printed invitations recently, and instead of putting this one task on my list, I separated it into designing the image, having the invitations printed, ordering stamps, and writing out the invitations. It was far less overwhelming, and I felt a sense of accomplishment after completing every step.

I can also recommend using flow charts, which allow you to map out processes and show you each step in a sequence, thereby reducing your cognitive load. Timers and reminders are helpful little nudges, too, keeping you on track without overwhelming you. Techniques such as time-blocking will also enhance your productivity. When you allocate specific time slots for tasks, you'll be able to create a routine that minimizes decision fatigue. A very mundane example of this from my own life is setting out my clothes for the next day in the evening. I do this every evening before dinner, and it's helped me to calm my mornings down. I used to spend far too long deliberating over what to wear, and I don't need that many decisions in the morning. When I've already sorted it out and given myself a routine block of time to do this, I find I'm so much less stressed out. No matter what you apply it to, this approach will help you to see the day as a series of manageable segments, each with a clear purpose and outcome.

There are digital tools that can help, too. Apps like Trello and Notion can help you organize your tasks visually, giving you a sense of control over your schedule and allowing you to prioritize your tasks using lists or boards. This makes it easier to visualize what's coming next, and there's a tremendous peace of mind to be found in this.

When you have several of these tools in place, you can create a structure that will help you manage your executive dysfunction by creating an external framework to support your internal processes. What you're essentially doing is building scaffolding around your tasks to make the things that feel complicated or overwhelming more approachable and achievable.

In the coming chapters, we'll look at these applications in more detail so that you can see how to use them in your quest for organization. The structure will ground you, providing a clear path forward even when you're faced with chaos, and you'll give yourself plenty of opportunity to celebrate small victories. For me, as someone who often felt like I was failing, this has been the most empowering part of the whole process.

Ultimately, managing executive dysfunction is about finding strategies that align with how your brain works. I'm not saying this doesn't require patience and experimentation, but if you commit to this, you can transform your approach to tasks and enhance your daily experience.

THE SCIENCE OF ADHD AND ORGANIZATION

Want to know why some tasks feel more challenging than they seem to for other people? It has to do with brain structure. People with ADHD often exhibit differences in the brain regions responsible for attention, planning, and impulse control, and these differences impact how you focus, plan, and execute tasks. The prefrontal cortex, for instance, is less active, affecting your ability to organize and prioritize. Your neurotransmitters are also important here. Dopamine, a neurotransmitter linked to reward and motivation, functions differently for people with ADHD, in whom the DRD_2 gene is defective, thereby making it harder for neurons to react to dopamine. This makes it harder for you to maintain focus on tasks that don't give you immediate gratification or excitement. When I first discovered this, it was like a lightbulb went on: There's a reason that organization doesn't come naturally to me! It also showed me what I could focus on in order to help myself, and I think this shows why targeted strategies can make such a significant difference.

Scientific research is a wonderful thing, and it has offered a range of strategies to help those of us with ADHD improve our organization. Cognitive behavioral techniques, for instance, have shown promise in helping us to manage task-related behaviors. These techniques encourage you to break down tasks into smaller, more manageable parts and use positive reinforcement to build new habits. Mindfulness practices have also been shown to be effective. Studies suggest that regular mindfulness exercises can enhance your ability to focus and regulate your emotions, which makes it easier for you to approach organizational tasks with clarity and calm. Mindfulness helps you to pause, assess your priorities, and act with intention rather than impulse. I'm not saying this is easy. When you're someone whose brain goes at 100 miles an hour, and distractions are plentiful, training yourself to be mindful can be a challenging task—but if I can do it, I have every confidence that you can, too. I started with guided meditations focused specifically on mindfulness. Apps like Headspace and Calm are a good starting point for this.

I find the interplay of ADHD traits and organizational skills fascinating, and it only takes a Google search to find stories about people who have leveraged their ADHD traits to improve their abilities to succeed or complete tasks. For example, some have found that their impulsivity, when channeled correctly, can lead to creative breakthroughs, and this is supported by research: Psychologists have discovered that people who believe that their impulsiveness benefits their creativity achieve a higher score on creative tasks. Rather than seeing impulsivity as a hindrance, they use it to drive innovation and adapt quickly to changing circumstances. So, your ADHD traits aren't necessarily obstacles; if you channel them well, they can be tools for success.

EMBRACING NEURODIVERSITY IN EVERYDAY TASKS

Neurodiversity is a term that acknowledges and celebrates the diversity of human brains and minds. It encourages us to recognize that variations in brain function are normal and that a difference is not a deficit. This is significant, especially in the context of ADHD, where we often feel pressured to conform to societal norms that don't align with our natural way of thinking. Neurodiversity sees ADHD as part of a spectrum where every brain is unique. Embracing these differences allows us to appreciate the varied ways in which people think, learn, and experience the world, and this, in turn, shifts the focus from trying to "fix" ADHD to understanding and valuing it.

What all of this means practically is that you'll need to tailor your routines to your individual strengths instead of forcing a one-size-fits-all approach onto yourself. This might mean rethinking how you organize your day—it certainly did for me. As you might have gleaned from the way I opened the book, I find mornings particularly challenging, and after years of fighting this, I decided to start my day a little later and try to ease myself into it gradually. I'm lucky enough to have the freedom in my schedule to allow this; you may find that you have challenges that make this more difficult, but if you think creatively, you may be able to find a solution. Perhaps you can't start your day any later, but what you can do is use your time differently. You might prepare the night before and use the time that you now have in the morning to take a walk or meditate for 20 minutes. It's a small change, but it could have a profound impact. Flexibility is the key here. Allow yourself to experiment with different methods until you find what works best. Maybe you can set up a flexible work schedule or use tools that cater to your unique processing style. The goal is to create routines that support your strengths and reduce your stress; this is how you're going to thrive.

We're lucky that we live in a world in which neurodiversity is becoming more widely accepted, and more and more workplaces are making an effort to create an inclusive environment. I hope you work somewhere like this, but even if you don't, you may find that you can make modifications that will be more supportive of your ADHD. Aim to minimize the number of distractions around you by using noise-canceling headphones or asking to switch desks with someone in a quieter space. You may also be able to play with your lighting and incorporate sensory elements that will help you find what feels comfortable for you. All of this can be done in your home environment, too. You might organize spaces to avoid sensory overload or create zones tailored to different activities. The changes you make will be personal to you, but they have the power to enhance your productivity and contribute to a sense of well-being. We'll dig deeper into strategies to improve your environment for enhanced organization and productivity as we move through the book.

Neurodiversity is less about you and more about our culture in general, and this means that advocacy and empowerment are important. If you feel comfortable sharing your experiences, I would encourage you to do this. You may be one voice, but one voice is a powerful thing, and it can raise awareness and help other people understand the challenges and strengths associated with ADHD. Consider starting conversations in your community or workplace, sharing stories that highlight the positive aspects of neurodiversity. Even if you don't feel comfortable with this quite yet, I'd encourage you to be an advocate for yourself, communicating your needs in order to create the best possible life for yourself. Perhaps this means requesting specific accommodations or explaining how ADHD affects your work style, even though I know this can be intimidating if you've tried to keep this part of yourself hidden for a long time. But ultimately, if you can develop these skills, you can build a more supportive environment and empower yourself to take control of your circumstances.

Reflection Time!

Take a moment to reflect on how neurodiversity plays a role in your life. Consider the following questions:

- What are three unique strengths that your ADHD brings to your everyday tasks?
- How can you adjust your routines to align with these strengths?
- What changes can you make in your environment to support your needs?
- How can you advocate for yourself in both a personal and a professional setting?

Write your thoughts in a journal or discuss them with someone you trust. For me, it was a journal, and it helped me to accept my neurodiversity and see it for what it is—a difference rather than a deficit.

The first step in accepting your ADHD and working with it rather than around it is celebrating what makes you unique. Focus on creating spaces and routines that support your natural way of being rather than trying to fit into a mold that doesn't suit you. Not to put any moral pressure on you, but this will not only enrich your life; it will also contribute to a more inclusive and understanding society, and this will make it easier for the generations that follow. Your unique brain is a strength, and I can honestly say that I really feel this about myself now. That isn't always something I could have claimed, and I feel so much freer and calmer now that I can.

2

MINDSET SHIFTS FOR SUCCESSFUL ORGANIZATION

The most powerful organizing strategy isn't found in a container store - it's discovered in the moment we stop fighting our ADHD brains and start collaborating with them.

I've always had to-do lists. I just haven't always had *effective* to-do lists. I used to wake up in the morning to find that my list had turned into a tangled web of unchecked boxes, and it seemed like each task was screaming at me. I used to think I was the only one who struggled with this, but many adults with ADHD face the daily challenge of organizing their lives amidst the chaos, and it's stressful. But what if these challenges were really just opportunities waiting to be discovered? I want to challenge your perception in this chapter and encourage you to see each challenge as a stepping stone toward growth and understanding. I've been able to change my perspective in this way, and it's transformed the way I approach my daily tasks.

TURNING CHALLENGES INTO OPPORTUNITIES

This process starts with reframing setbacks. I want to ask you to see each stumble as a chance to learn and improve rather than as a failure. Reflect on your past experiences. Can you think of times when things didn't go as you planned? What lessons did they teach you? Perhaps an overlooked deadline taught you the value of setting reminders, or maybe a cluttered workspace highlighted your need for a more structured environment. I know these experiences are often highly frustrating, but they also hold valuable insights that can inform your future actions—and if you can view it that way, I think you'll find it extremely liberating.

ADHD traits offer unique opportunities for creative problem-solving. Your brain is wired differently, and it's adept at seeing connections that other people might miss. This can be a powerful asset when tackling organizational tasks. Spontaneous bursts of creativity can be channeled into innovative solutions. Perhaps you've found unconventional ways to streamline your workspace or devised a unique system for managing tasks that suit your personal rhythm. These creative approaches simultaneously solve your immediate problems and build confidence in your ability to navigate complex challenges. I encourage you to embrace the unexpected insights your

Developing resilience is essential in overcoming organizational hurdles. Resilience is the mental fortitude that allows you to persevere through adversity, emerging stronger and more capable. It doesn't mean you won't face difficulties, but it does mean that you'll have the strength to rise above them, learning and growing with each experience.

Reflection Time!

Take a moment to reflect on a recent challenge you faced. Consider the following questions:

- What specific lessons did this challenge teach you?
- How can you apply these lessons to future tasks?
- What strengths did you discover in yourself while overcoming this challenge?
- How can you creatively leverage your ADHD traits in similar situations?

Again, write out your thoughts or talk about them with someone you trust to reinforce the idea that challenges are opportunities for growth and self-discovery.

It will be gradual, but as you adopt this mindset, you'll begin to transform your perception of challenges and slowly come to see them as opportunities.

CULTIVATING A GROWTH MINDSET WITH ADHD

You've probably come across the ideas of a growth mindset and a fixed mindset before. The idea, developed by psychologist Carol Dweck, suggests that individuals with a growth mindset believe intelligence and talents can be cultivated through effort and learning. In contrast, a fixed mindset assumes that these traits are innate and unchangeable. For those with ADHD, I believe that adopting a growth-oriented perspective can be transformative. I used to think I was a lost cause and that there wasn't anything I could do to improve my organization, timekeeping, or ability to focus, but I've been able to turn my perceived limitations into areas ripe for development. Nothing has changed except my mindset. The growth mindset empowers you to see challenges as opportunities to learn and improve rather than as roadblocks to success. It can be cultivated... but it takes daily effort.

You want to start by setting both realistic and stretch goals. Realistic goals are achievable and encouraging stepping stones, while stretch goals challenge you to push beyond your comfort zone and current capabilities. For example, if organizing paperwork is a struggle for you, a realistic goal might be to sort one folder a day, while a stretch goal might be to organize the entire desk by the end of the week. Taken on a surface level, this isn't something I'd recommend to someone with ADHD, but cast your mind back to the to-do lists and how satisfying it is to include every small sub-task in them. A stretch goal can be managed like that. If you write "Organize my whole desk by Friday" on your to-do list, you're unlikely to achieve the goal... but if you dissect every part of that process and spread it out through the week, you *will* be able to achieve it.

Part of building a growth mindset is changing your perception of failure. We're conditioned to see failure through a negative lens, but each one has the potential to teach us. Rather than viewing setbacks with self-criticism, choose to see them as valuable learning experiences. Analyze what went wrong, identify the lessons, and apply them to your future endeavors. Over time, this will reduce your fear of failure and encourage you to experiment and innovate. Encourage yourself to take on a problem-solving attitude, which will help you to turn hurdles into opportunities. Whenever I'm faced with an obstacle (which is often!), I break it down into manageable parts, brainstorm solutions, and test different approaches. It's made me see each challenge as a puzzle that I get to solve, and this has built my resilience and forced me to lean into my creativity. I wasn't always like this, believe me, and if I can shift my thinking like this, you can too.

Did you know that there are techniques to help you with mindset transformation? You don't just have to pull this out of nowhere, and I promise you, I didn't. Daily affirmations are a powerful tool for me; they help me reinforce positive beliefs, subtly reprogramming my subconscious to embrace growth. I'd recommend starting each day with affirmations that align with your goals. Two that have been very effective for me are "I am capable of learning and growing" and "Every challenge is an opportunity." They remind me of my potential, even on days when I feel like I'm failing. I've also used visualization exercises to great effect. I imagine myself achieving my goal, picturing each step I'll take in detail and seeing myself enjoying my success. This is basically mental rehearsal, and it has the power to increase your motivation and confidence, which will make the path to success clearer and more attainable.

Embracing the concept of growth allows you to unlock the potential that's already inside you, and it can transform how you approach both personal and professional tasks. The growth mindset encourages continuous learning, resilience, and adaptability, and these are essential qualities when it comes to navigating life with ADHD. Remember, though, that change takes time. Be patient with yourself, and celebrate every step forward, no matter how small it seems. Your potential is boundless, and with a growth mindset, you'll be well-equipped to explore it.

EMPOWERMENT THROUGH SELF-DISCOVERY

When you become aware of your personal strengths, you can tailor your approach to organizing tasks. Perhaps you're adept at visual thinking, which could translate into creating detailed and colorful mind maps to help you organize your thoughts. Maybe you have a knack for seeing the big picture, which might help you to prioritize your tasks effectively. If you can acknowledge and understand these strengths, you can leverage them in ways that align with your natural inclinations, and this will make the organization feel less like a chore and more like a personal triumph. There's a catch, though: You'll also have to recognize areas where you might struggle. This isn't about labeling weaknesses, and I'd encourage you not to see it that way; it's about finding opportunities for targeted improvement. If you find it challenging to stay focused, for example, you might explore techniques that cater to your cognitive style, such as using timers to maintain attention or breaking tasks into smaller, manageable parts.

There are plenty of tools out there designed to help us understand ourselves, and they can be very helpful in the quest for self-discovery. Personality assessments, for example, can tell you more about how your mind works. They may reveal patterns in how you approach problems, handle stress, or prefer to communicate, which will tell you more about how you can design your life to suit your needs. They may give you a framework for understanding your organizational style, and this will help you craft strategies that resonate with you.

Journaling is a powerful tool for reflective thinking, too. By writing about your daily experiences, you can uncover recurring themes, thoughts, and behaviors. I was never a big diarist, but I started doing this specifically for this purpose, and it's been helpful. I use prompts to help me, which I generally come up with myself, simply to give me a focus. In this case, you might ask yourself something like, "What organizational task felt most natural today?" or "Where did I face the most resistance?" The danger for me, if I don't have a prompt, is that I'll get distracted and end up on a totally different topic; prompts like this will guide your reflection so that you can find the clarity and insight you're looking for. Over time, you'll deepen your self-awareness and build a sense of agency and empowerment. As you document your experiences, you'll begin to see patterns and uncover hidden strengths, and this will pave the way for personal growth and development.

Aligning your strengths with tasks is a strategic way to enhance your productivity and satisfaction. When you match tasks to your cognitive strengths, they often seem more manageable and less daunting. For example, if you're a natural planner, organizing complex projects might become an enjoyable challenge rather than a source of stress. On the other hand, if you struggle with detail-oriented tasks, you might be better off delegating them when you can or using tools that simplify the process, such as checklists or apps that track progress. I'd like to remind you at this point that delegating tasks that don't align with your skills isn't a sign of weakness; it's a strategic decision that frees you up to focus on what you do best. When you align your strengths with your responsibilities, you can both enhance your efficiency and boost your confidence and satisfaction with your work, which will give you a sense of purpose and fulfillment.

I think that consciously committing to continuous self-growth is vital to maintaining this momentum. You can't really take your eye off the ball, and the best way to make sure you don't is to set personal development goals that challenge and inspire you. They could really be anything—mastering a new skill or improving an existing one; whatever it is, it's contributing to your long-term growth. Every goal is a benchmark for progress, and it offers you the gift of direction and motivation. Engage in lifelong learning opportunities (like workshops, courses, or reading) to enrich your journey of self-discovery. Embrace a mindset of curiosity and openness, seeking out experiences that stretch your understanding and capabilities. It may seem like a curve ball, but personal growth is always valuable, and it cultivates resilience, adaptability, and a deeper understanding of yourself and the world around you.

OVERCOMING NEGATIVE SELF-PERCEPTION

Living with ADHD often means dealing with a running commentary in your mind that can be less than kind. At least, this has been my experience, and I know that negative self-talk is a familiar adversary for many people. It whispers doubts about your abilities and worth, and it leads you to believe in a narrative that can be hard to shake yourself free from. If you recognize these patterns in yourself, you've already taken the first step toward changing them. The thoughts, "I can't keep anything organized," or "I'm always messing things up," used to be common ones for me, and they undermined my confidence and impacted my ability to manage tasks effectively. The danger is that when you internalize this negativity, it not only affects your perception of yourself but also hinders your organizational abilities. Every single task feels heavier when you're constantly battling thoughts like this, but if you can identify them, you can begin to see them for what they are —just thoughts, not truths.

What you're going to have to do is replace your negative inner dialogue with supportive affirmations. You'll need to make a conscious effort to speak to yourself with the same kindness and understanding that you'd offer a friend. One thing I found helpful, every time I caught myself judging myself harshly, was to think about my best friend and ask myself, "Would I ever say this to her?" The answer was always no, and it was an eye-opening exercise.

It won't necessarily be easy at first, but I'd recommend starting each day with affirmations that reinforce your strengths and potential. Simple statements like "I am capable of organizing my space" or "I have the skills to succeed" can make a significant difference if you use them often. Over time, your affirmations will become a part of your mental landscape, and they'll help you to shift your self-perception from doubt to confidence.

You also want to pay attention to your social network. Surround yourself with people who uplift you and see your potential even when you struggle to see it yourself. Their belief in you can act as a powerful counterbalance to the negative self-talk, helping you to build a more positive and resilient self-image. The more open you can be with these people, the better. If you feel those negative thoughts coming in and you feel at liberty to share them, you'll likely be given positive affirmations in return. Pay attention to them. They're not just cookie-cutter responses; they mean something, and the people saying them really believe them.

Challenging limiting beliefs requires a conscious effort to question and reframe the thoughts that hold you back. Cognitive restructuring exercises can be a valuable tool in this process. When you catch yourself in a spiral of negative thinking, pause and ask yourself, "Is this thought based on fact, or is it a reflection of my fear?" When you examine the evidence for and against these beliefs, you can begin to dismantle them. Again, journaling might help you here. Document these moments and the alternative perspectives you discover and use these reflections to help you guide yourself toward a more positive mindset.

If your negative thoughts are very overbearing, you may find that professional support is necessary. Therapists and coaches are trained to provide guidance and strategies that will help you, and they can offer an external perspective that may illuminate alternatives you hadn't considered. Seeking help is never a sign of weakness; it's a proactive step toward growth and self-improvement.

I want to draw your attention, at this point, to Justin Lafond, who's known for his work in ADHD advocacy, particularly focusing on how individuals with ADHD can harness their unique skills and challenges to achieve career success. He transformed his hyperfocus from a source of frustration into a strength that propelled him through his academic pursuits and into a successful career. His approach often emphasizes the importance of self-awareness, tailored organizational strategies, and leveraging creative thinking as strengths in the workplace, and, for me, he's a huge inspiration. His journey highlights how changing the narrative around ADHD can lead to personal and professional success.

Overcoming negative self-perception is a gradual process, and it means tuning in to the internal dialogue that undermines your confidence. Only then will you be able to build a positive self-image, and from here, you'll be able to come up with practical strategies that will allow you to build on this foundation and move toward a more organized and fulfilling life.

3

CREATING A FOUNDATION FOR ORGANIZATION

Between the chaos and the calm lies a bridge built from self-understanding. Your ADHD brain already knows what it needs - we're just going to give it the building blocks to make it happen.

I think a mistake that a lot of people make when it comes to organization is starting with the organization itself. If that's something that you struggle with, it's going to be very difficult unless you have a strong foundation in place to begin with, and that's what we'll concentrate on in this chapter.

BUILDING A ROUTINE THAT WORKS FOR YOU

I'd guess that the mornings that you wake up with a sense of calm anticipation and know exactly how your day will unfold are few and far between, but that's what we're striving for. You want to find a rhythm, a predictability that can guide you through the chaos without feeling monotonous. Having a consistent routine has been so important to me. It provides a framework around which I can build my day, giving me both stability and a sense of control. If you can build something like this, it will help you to manage the ebb and flow of your energy levels, and this will enable you to allocate your resources efficiently.

I think morning routines are the most important part of the equation because they set the tone for the rest of the day. Start with small rituals that ground you. What these are is entirely up to you; maybe it's a moment of mindfulness, a quick stretch, or simply enjoying a cup of coffee without any distractions. Any one of these practices will help you to center your thoughts and allow you to build into the day slowly and smoothly. Evening wind-down routines are helpful, too. They signal to your brain that it's time to relax and prepare for rest. Again, what you do is really up to you, but activities like reading, gentle yoga, or listening to calming music are popular choices for easing the mind and reducing the clutter of thoughts that often accompanies bedtime. Calming evening routines like this promote better sleep and provide a sense of closure to the day, giving you an opportunity to reflect and recharge.

What you don't want to do is blindly follow a routine that works for someone else without considering whether it will really suit you. You want to customize your routines so that they fit your personal lifestyle and preferences. Energy levels often vary when you have ADHD. You may be familiar with fatigue and exhaustion, especially at the end of the day, but if you think about how much energy goes into hyperactivity, hyperfocus, and anxiety, this makes sense. Some days, you might feel like you can conquer the world, and on others, even the simplest tasks are daunting. This is something that used to really irritate me about myself, but I made a conscious choice to work on acceptance, and it's made a world of difference because it allows me to structure my days in a way that supports me rather than trying to fight my own needs all the time. Embrace the fluctuation in your energy levels by creating routines that will adapt as you need them to. On low-energy days, focus on "non-negotiables," the essential tasks that keep your life running smoothly. On days when you have a lot of energy, you can tackle "extra credit" tasks, those that go above and beyond but aren't necessary to your everyday functioning.

If you struggle to keep your attention on things that don't interest you, the trick is to *make* them interesting. Try to incorporate your personal interests into your routine to help you stay engaged. If you love music, for instance, use it as a motivator while you're doing mundane tasks. If you feel under-stimulated at home and you have tasks you could do elsewhere, try taking them to a coffee shop or a library. If you have particular interests, try to find podcasts that you can listen to while you're working through mindless tasks. These are all tiny adjustments, but they can make your routines feel less like a chore, and you're more likely to find enjoyment in them.

The next challenge you have is making sure that you can maintain your routines over time, and to do this, you'll need to be intentional. Habit-tracking tools and apps help a lot of people because they provide visual cues that reinforce consistency. They give you a tangible way to see your progress because they have the effect of turning abstract goals into something concrete. Having accountability partners in the form of friends or family is helpful, too. They will offer you support and encouragement and help you to stay committed when your motivation is waning. Life is unpredictable, and your routines will need to adapt to reflect this. The secret to this, in my experience, is to evaluate and adjust them regularly—otherwise, you may find yourself going through the motions of routines that are no longer relevant to where you are in your life or following along with ones that aren't that effective. If you review your routines periodically, you'll be able to assess what's working and what isn't, and this will give you the opportunity to refine your approach.

For me, one of the challenges with this process has been being honest with myself. My journal has come in handy here. I made a habit of noting the days when my routines felt seamless and the days when they didn't. Doing this regularly helped me to see the rusty days as less of a failure than I had previously felt them to be, and this encouraged me to be more honest about it with myself. I'd advise trying this method, looking for patterns and barriers that are making it difficult for you to stick to your routines. Perhaps certain tasks consistently disrupt your flow, or maybe external factors, like unexpected obligations, throw you off course. If you can identify these, you can address these barriers and pave the way for more effective routines. Perhaps you change the times at which you complete certain tasks, maybe you take more breaks, or maybe it's just a matter of simplifying your approach.

Reflection Time!

Create a checklist to assess your current routines. Ask yourself the following questions:

- Does my routine fit my current lifestyle and energy levels?
- Are there tasks that consistently disrupt my flow?
- What adjustments can I make to improve the effectiveness of my routine?
- How can I incorporate my personal interests so that I stay more engaged?

Use this checklist periodically to refine your routines, ensuring they continue to support your organizational goals.

PERSONALIZED TIME MANAGEMENT STRATEGIES

Time often feels elusive to me, and this is a common experience for people with ADHD. You might find yourself constantly battling time blindness, that peculiar sensation where minutes slip away unnoticed, leaving you scrambling to catch up. This phenomenon, which we often dismiss as "losing track of time," has to do with how ADHD affects our perception of time. Tasks that seem urgent can overshadow those that are truly important, and this often leads us into a cycle of prioritizing the immediate over the strategic. What this has meant for me in the past is that because there's *always* something that seems to be immediately important, the tasks that would be sensible to prioritize from a strategic point of view just never happened. I had to learn to differentiate urgency from importance, and once I was able to do this, I could allocate my time more effectively, which meant that my long-term goals didn't get lost in the shuffle of daily demands.

Time-blocking can help you with this. The goal is to assign specific blocks of time to different activities, covering every part of your day, which essentially turns an abstract to-do list into a visual map of your day. To boost the effect of this even further, you can use color-coded calendars, which will provide visual clarity and help you quickly identify what tasks demand your attention. For instance, you might use blue for work-related tasks, green for personal projects, and red for urgent deadlines. Don't forget to schedule breaks into the mix. These will prevent burnout and offer your brain a chance to reset, which, although it might feel counterintuitive when you have a lot to get done, will improve your overall productivity. It doesn't need to be long; it could be a five-minute pause to stretch or take a quick walk around the block. Regular breaks will give your day a rhythm and help you maintain your focus when you return to your tasks.

You don't need to do all of this on your own—as they say, there's an app for that! You can use digital planners and reminder systems like Google Calendar or Todoist, which are designed to help you keep track of tasks and deadlines. They provide reminders and alerts so that nothing slips through the cracks.

You can also use techniques like the Pomodoro Technique, which involves working in focused bursts, typically 25 minutes, followed by a short break. This is great if you tend to hyperfocus because it allows you to channel it into productive work sessions. By dividing tasks into manageable intervals, you can maintain concentration and make steady progress throughout the day, which will improve your productivity and instill a sense of accomplishment as you tick off completed intervals.

There is a trap here, however. You don't want so much structure that you're unable to accommodate changes when life demands them. Time management is only sustainable when you're able to balance flexibility and structure. Schedules do provide a framework, but life often throws unexpected situations our way, and we need to be able to adjust our plans in response to spontaneous opportunities. Maybe a friend invites you to lunch, or a sudden work deadline shifts your priorities. Building buffer time into your daily schedule can accommodate these changes. The goal is to create a schedule that serves you—not the other way around. If you can strike this balance, your day will feel manageable and less rigid, and it will accommodate both the activities you planned for and any spontaneous moments that come up.

Reflection Time!

Consider these questions as you evaluate your time management strategies:

- How does time blindness affect your daily activities?
- What color-coding system might work for your time-blocking?
- How can you incorporate breaks to improve your focus and prevent burnout?
- Where could you include buffer time to allow for flexibility?

Reflect on your answers and use them to refine your approach to managing time.

SETTING ACHIEVABLE GOALS AND OBJECTIVES

Setting goals is often daunting for people with ADHD because of the way our brains process information and prioritize tasks. We can, however, get around this by using structured frameworks like SMART goals, which can give us a clear, focused path forward. SMART stands for Specific, Measurable, Achievable, Relevant, and Time-bound, and these criteria help us to keep our goals realistic and clearly defined. I'd heard so much about SMART goals over the years that I was almost resistant to using them, but I have to say, they feel like a map to me, and they help me to guide my actions and decisions.

Let's take the example of decluttering a room in your home to illustrate how a SMART goal might work:

- **Specific:** I will declutter my bedroom by sorting all items into keep, donate, and discard categories.
- **Measurable:** I will complete this task by removing at least 50 items that I no longer use or need.
- **Achievable:** I will set aside two hours every Saturday for the next four weeks to achieve this goal.

- **Relevant:** Decluttering my bedroom will create a more organized and peaceful space, contributing to my overall well-being and productivity.
- **Time-bound:** I will complete the decluttering process in 4 weeks (make sure to include the specific date).

You'll also want to differentiate between short-term and long-term goals. Short-term goals act as stepping stones, immediate milestones that keep you motivated and engaged. Long-term goals represent the broader objectives you want to achieve. You might have a long-term goal to create an organized home environment and a short-term goal to declutter one room per week. Setting your goals in this way will allow you to break down larger objectives into manageable tasks, and it will give you a sense of accomplishment as you progress. It's the small victories that give you momentum, and they'll make the journey toward your larger aspirations feel less daunting and more attainable.

Aligning your goals with your personal values is how you'll make sure that they resonate with your true desires and motivations. Take a moment to think about what truly matters to you. Is it creativity, family, or personal growth? When you have a clear idea of your values, you can prioritize goals that align with them so that your efforts feel meaningful and fulfilling. Goals that resonate with your personal ambitions are more likely to inspire motivation and perseverance, and this will make it easier to overcome obstacles and challenges along the way.

To make sure you stay on course, you're going to need to track and measure your progress, and to do this, I'd recommend visual tools like goal-tracking boards and charts so that you have a tangible representation of your achievements. You'll be able to see how far you've come, and this will reinforce your commitment to your objectives. Schedule time to assess your achievements, celebrate milestones, and adjust your plans as you need to. This will keep you accountable and help you to adapt to any changes or setbacks that come up. Celebrating milestones, no matter how small, reinforces positive behaviors and boosts motivation. Maybe you treat yourself to indulging in a favorite activity or acknowledge your efforts with a small reward; whatever you do to celebrate, you'll create a positive feedback loop that will encourage you to keep making progress.

By setting achievable goals and aligning them with your values, you'll create a foundation for success that resonates with your needs and aspirations. Patience and perseverance are going to be key. Embrace each step forward and allow yourself to learn and grow with each experience.

4

STRATEGIES FOR DECLUTTERING YOUR SPACE

Each item we release isn't just clearing physical space - it's making room for your ADHD mind to breathe, create, and thrive in an environment that finally feels like it was designed for you.

What does it feel like when you walk into your home after a long day? Are you greeted by piles of clutter that seem to grow every time you turn your back? Trust me, I'm familiar with those monster piles, as are many people with ADHD. The thing about clutter is that it isn't just physical; it seeps into your mind and affects your focus and mood. I know how overwhelming the idea of decluttering can be when it's been building up for a long time, but it's easier than you may think. The secret is to start small, with quick wins that build your confidence and motivate you to keep going. In this chapter, we'll look at strategies that offer immediate satisfaction, which will make the daunting task of decluttering feel both achievable and rewarding.

QUICK WINS TO BOOST YOUR CONFIDENCE

I'd recommend focusing on immediate impact areas first. These are the spaces you encounter daily, like entryways and common areas. Imagine the difference it would make to step into a tidy hallway instead of tripping over shoes and bags. I cleaned up my hallway first, and even though it was a while before I got around to anything else, it made a huge difference to my peace of mind. Just coming in the front door, seeing a clutter-free carpet, and taking a deep breath was so soothing in contrast to my previous experience (which generally involved piles of unopened mail, collections of things I intended to take upstairs, and a flock of shoes that badly needed organizing). If you address these high-traffic zones first, you'll create a sense of order that will greet you every time you enter your home.

Your next priority should be the surfaces where you work, like desks or kitchen counters. These areas influence your daily productivity and mood. If an average workday feels like a battle, I'm certain that cleaning your desk up will help it to feel like a fresh start instead, and it will boost your mental clarity and focus. This made such a big difference to me.

You might only have a few minutes to spare, but you can still get some quick results. Start with a five-minute pickup routine. Set a timer and focus on visible surfaces, quickly removing anything that's out of place. You'll be surprised at how much order you can restore in such a short time. Often, we look at the whole picture, and it becomes impossible to see how we can make any progress in the amount of time we have, but it's usually this thought process that's standing in our way.

You might also want to try the "one-in, one-out" rule. For every new item you bring into your space, choose one to remove. This will help you to keep the buildup of clutter under control and encourage you to be mindful of what you acquire.

You might be surprised by the psychological benefits of achieving quick wins in decluttering. Every small success builds momentum, and this will reinforce your belief in your ability to create change. No matter how small the victory, celebrate it. Treat yourself to your favorite meal or take a relaxing bath—whatever makes you feel good and allows you to recognize your success. To boost your motivation and accountability even more, try sharing before-and-after photos with friends or on social media. When you can see tangible evidence of your progress, you'll feel more confident in your abilities and be spurred on to continue. Each one of your small wins will build toward the more significant changes you make further down the line, and every one of them is important.

When I first started with quick decluttering tasks like this, I found it hard to see how I was going to make much progress, but it really did set a positive tone for the larger projects that came later. The little tasks demonstrated that transformation was possible, even though it felt like it was out of reach, and I'd really encourage you to take this approach. Consider setting daily decluttering challenges to keep you engaged and enthusiastic. Maybe you challenge yourself to clear out a single drawer or organize a small corner of the living room; perhaps you decide to weed out all the clothes you don't wear anymore. Whatever you do, as you build the habit of regular tidying, the prospect of tackling bigger projects will become less daunting, and over time, you'll acquire ingrained habits, which will build a cycle of continuous improvement that extends beyond your physical space and enhances your overall well-being.

Before-and-After Photo Challenge

Take a "before" photo of a cluttered area in your home. Spend 15 minutes tidying and organizing it, and then snap an "after" photo. Compare the two. Share them with a friend or on social media as a way to celebrate your progress and inspire others to do the same thing. Pay attention to how this small change impacts your mood and motivation; I think you'll be pleasantly surprised.

STEP-BY-STEP DECLUTTERING HACKS

If your house looks anything like mine did before I began this process, even standing in your living room contemplating decluttering might be overwhelming. This is where a systematic approach is helpful; it will make it seem more manageable, perhaps even liberating. Start by creating a room-by-room roadmap. This will allow you to focus on one space at a time and make sure that each area receives the care and attention it deserves. Begin with the spaces you frequent the most, where clutter might disrupt your daily activities. As you move through each room, categorize items by type and frequency of use. This will help you to understand what truly matters to you, as well as make the organization process easier. I can almost guarantee that you'll find many items serve little purpose, and this will make it easier to decide what to keep and what to let go of.

There are also some practical decluttering techniques that will help you. The "four-box method" is one of the first ones you'll come across on any downsizing or home organization blog. The principle is simple. You divide your belongings into four categories: Keep, Donate, Sell, and Trash. As you sort, consider the value each item brings to your life. If it's something you use daily or that holds significant sentimental value, it goes in the *Keep* box.

Items that no longer serve you but are in good condition can be added to the *Donate* or *Sell* boxes, and you'll feel good knowing that someone else will benefit from them. Your *Trash* box, obviously, is for the things that are beyond repair or use, and you might be surprised by how much of this category you've accumulated.

Once you've sorted your item, your next job is to assign designated spaces for frequently used items so that everything has a home and there's less likelihood of the clutter returning. I like to use labeling systems so that I can easily find what I'm looking for, which saves a lot of time and frustration, and I know that visual cues like this are very helpful for many other people with ADHD.

Incorporating ADHD-friendly methods into your decluttering strategy is going to be key to your success. Visual cues will prompt you to take action when you might otherwise be distracted. I use a combination of color-coded bins and sticky notes to remind me what needs attention. I also break tasks into smaller, more digestible steps, so instead of tackling an entire room, I focus on one section, like a drawer or a shelf. I've tried focusing on the whole room, and it doesn't work for me. I get overwhelmed, and my momentum wanes quickly. If you divide larger projects into bite-sized pieces, you'll set yourself up for a series of small victories that will build your confidence and motivation. Every task you complete will reinforce your belief in your ability to manage your space, and what once felt like chaos will become a source of empowerment and pride. Believe me, if I found this, you will too!

Be patient with yourself as you go through this process. Sentimental items can be challenging to deal with. The memories and emotions they carry can make them difficult to part with, and you may struggle with this even if you feel that holding onto them isn't the right decision. One thing you could do is to set aside a specific space for sentimental items, somewhere that will allow you to preserve them without contributing to everyday clutter. You could also consider taking photographs of these items as a way to cherish the memories without holding onto the physical object.

You may find that you struggle with decision fatigue as the process goes on. To combat this, set time limits for decision-making, as suggested by organizing expert Judith Kolberg Kolberg, 2024). Having a constraint like this will encourage you to trust your instincts and make decisions more quickly. You could also ask for help from a "clutter companion," which is really just a new title for a friend or family member. Sometimes, an outside perspective is really very valuable, and it may help you see beyond the emotional attachment and focus on your goals.

USING THE POMODORO TECHNIQUE FOR DECLUTTERING

It's all very well setting aside time to declutter, but the chances are you'll find your focus waning after a few minutes. This is a common experience for adults with ADHD, and if this is something that happens to you, the Pomodoro Technique we discussed earlier might be the game-changer you're looking for. Originally developed by Francesco Cirillo as a time-management tool in the 1980s, it involves setting a 25-minute timer for focused work periods, followed by short breaks. You can adapt this method to suit decluttering by creating structured intervals that will help you maintain attention without feeling overwhelmed. Start with a timer set for 25 minutes—a Pomodoro session—during which time you'll be focused on tidying up. When the timer rings, step away from the task and take a five-minute break to recharge. Following this cycle will reduce the risk of burnout and allow you to return to your task with renewed energy and focus.

To implement the Pomodoro Technique effectively, make sure you identify specific areas or items to focus on for each session. Choose a drawer, a section of your closet, or a single shelf. By targeting your approach this way, you'll be able to tackle the clutter in manageable chunks, which will make the process feel less daunting. Try to evaluate your accomplishments as you progress through each Pomodoro session. Did you clear the space you intended? If not, what obstacles did you encounter? These are the questions that will help you adjust your strategy for the next session and learn from the process. Tracking your progress might feel like an unnecessary extra step, but when I've done this, I've found that it's given me a sense of accomplishment and shown me where I could streamline my efforts in order to see better results.

It's common for people with ADHD to have problems with time perception, and timed sessions can significantly boost your efficiency if this is an issue for you. I find that the ticking timer acts as a gentle reminder and keeps me focused on the present task without my mind wandering. As you complete each Pomodoro, acknowledge it as a success so that you have tangible evidence of your progress, which will reinforce your belief in your ability to manage time effectively. You don't need to stick strictly to the original Pomodoro model, either. You can adjust the length of your sessions according to your personal focus levels. If 25 minutes feels too long or too short, experiment with different durations. All that matters is that you find a balance that keeps you engaged without leading to fatigue.

You can boost the effectiveness of the Pomodoro Technique by pairing it with other decluttering strategies like the "Four-box method" we discussed earlier. During each Pomodoro, focus on sorting items into four categories: Keep, Donate, Sell, and Trash. You may find that it will help you to make your decisions more quickly and confidently. You could also use the Pomodoro Technique to tackle particularly challenging areas. If you have a room or a closet that feels overwhelming, break it into smaller sections, dedicating a Pomodoro to each. This should make it seem less intimidating.

Personalized Pomodoro Planner

Create a simple planner to track your Pomodoro sessions. Divide a page into the following sections:

- Task
- Pomodoros Planned
- Pomodoros Completed
- Challenges Faced
- Adjustments Made

Use this planner to plan and evaluate each session, making notes on what works and what needs improvement. This will help you to refine your approach and make sure that each session is productive and rewarding.

MAINTAINING A CLUTTER-FREE ZONE

Once you've tackled the initial clutter, the real challenge begins: keeping it at bay. Your best strategy here will be to establish maintenance routines to prevent the chaos from creeping back. Your goal is to create daily rituals that will keep your space (and mind) clear. Focus on high-use areas. It's amazing how effective a quick sweep through the kitchen or living room each day can be. Spend just a few minutes every day returning items to their designated spots, and you'll be surprised by how easy it is to manage. Your week can also include deeper cleaning, in which you address areas that need more attention. Perhaps you dedicate an hour to a specific task like dusting or vacuuming on the weekend. You may not love the idea at first, but if you can integrate these tasks into your schedule, you'll start to see them as habits rather than chores.

For me, habits have been essential to maintaining a clutter-free lifestyle, but it does take a bit of patience and commitment at the beginning. After all, no habit is built overnight. To make it easier for you to adopt a habit, consider habit stacking, a technique where you link new habits to established ones. You might, for example, take a moment to organize the kitchen counter while you're waiting for your morning coffee to brew. By attaching the task to something else you're doing already, you'll be able to build a routine that will become second nature over time.

I've also found it helpful to set reminders for regular organization check-ins. I have an alert on my phone to prompt me to evaluate my space, and this helps me to make sure that clutter doesn't accumulate without me noticing. Otherwise, I find that things can spiral out of control very quickly, but by taking these small, consistent actions, I've established a rhythm that keeps my space tidy and my mind calm.

You can also design your spaces so that they naturally resist clutter accumulation. Implement storage solutions that align with your lifestyle needs. It's worth thinking about multifunctional furniture that will provide extra storage without taking up additional space. Ottomans or coffee tables with hidden compartments are good for this, and you can also get storage beds and couches. The more accessible storage you have, the less likely it is that you'll be tempted to leave items out, and this will help you minimize the buildup of clutter. You could also arrange your furniture to create clear pathways and designate specific areas of the room for different activities. Do this well, and you can improve the flow of your space while reducing the chances of clutter accumulating in unintended places. If you think about the design of your home as well as clearing up the clutter that already exists, you can establish an environment that supports your organizational goals, essentially making your space work for you rather than against you.

To ensure continuous improvement and adaptation, consider incorporating feedback loops into your decluttering practices. All I really mean by this is evaluating your process regularly so that you can identify areas that need attention or adjustment. Set aside time each month to review your space and consider what's working well and where you might need to make changes. You could even share your progress with accountability partners like friends, family members, or support groups. Again, these people will be able to offer you a fresh perspective and help you to identify your blind spots and celebrate your successes.

In the end, maintaining a clutter-free zone is about consistency and mindfulness. Success lies in creating habits and environments that support your goals and enhance your well-being. Remember that one thing may not necessarily work forever; it's a dynamic process, and it should evolve with you and your needs. This is your foundation, but I'm very aware that there are particular challenges we face when we live with ADHD, and we need to have strategies we can use to overcome them. This is what we'll look at in the next chapter.

5

ENHANCING FOCUS AND REDUCING DISTRACTIONS

Between the notifications pinging, the ideas flowing, and the world's constant motion, there's a sweet spot where your ADHD mind can thrive. Let's find your path to that space.

Are your spaces really designed for you, or do they reflect a pattern you've followed without really thinking about it? I can tell you that, for a long time, mine were the latter. I didn't really think about *why* I arranged them the way I did; in fact, I put very little thought into it at all. But if you walk into a room designed just for you—a place where focus comes naturally and distractions are minimized—you'll have a space that will work with you to keep it organized. This is the heart of what it means to create a focus-friendly environment, and it's especially helpful for those of us with ADHD.

CREATING FOCUS-FRIENDLY ENVIRONMENTS

Right now, your space might be cluttered with unfinished tasks and objects that constantly demand your attention, but no matter how chaotic it feels, you can transform it into one that supports your need for concentration, allows your mind to settle, and minimizes the chances of distraction when you're trying to focus.

This can be done in any room, but let's start with your desk space as an example. First of all, you need to think about the overall design of the whole room. How you arrange your furniture can influence your mental state. If your desk is cluttered, your mind is going to be cluttered, and this isn't just about the desk itself—it's also about what you can see when you're sitting at it. You want to aim to reduce visual distractions by arranging your furniture in a way that feels open and unencumbered. This might mean removing unnecessary items from the desk itself, but it might also mean thinking about where that desk is. If it's currently against a wall, you might want to reposition it to face a window, which will allow natural light to invigorate your senses. Think about this carefully, though. If you're likely to be distracted by what goes on outside your window, a better choice might be to keep it somewhere where it gets the light without requiring you to look out. I tried to position mine so it looked out of the window, but I quickly moved it because I was getting distracted by cats, birds, the weather—you name it! Now I have it facing a wall but close to the window, and that's a far better fit for me. Noise is another persistent intruder for people with ADHD, and it can increase your symptoms of inattentiveness. The world is full of sounds that can shatter concentration —your neighbor's dog barking, the hum of the refrigerator, distant chatter in the street… Noise-canceling headphones are good for blocking out these background noises and calming your auditory landscape so you can focus, and they'd be a great addition to your desk drawer if noise is often a problem for you.

Tailoring your environment to work with your sensory preferences will enhance your focus by aligning your space with the things that soothe and motivate you. Consider the colors that surround you. Calming hues like blues and greens can create a serene backdrop that promotes concentration, while harsh, bright colors might overstimulate you. If your desk space is currently in a room with dark or bright colors, you may wish to consider freshening up the paint. Your lighting is important, too. Opt for natural light whenever you can, which you can then supplement during darker hours with strategically placed lamps. Soft, diffused lighting can reduce eye strain and create a peaceful atmosphere, and this is where the color temperature of a light bulb comes in. Bulbs between 2700K and 3000K are lower color temperatures, and they're warmer and a softer yellow color. Bulbs between 4000K and 65000K have higher color temperatures and emit a cooler light that's bluer in its tone. In a workspace, a balance of the two is best for creating a peaceful atmosphere with minimal eye strain. It's worth thinking about the textures and materials in your environment as well. Soft fabrics, warm woods, or smooth stones can offer tactile comfort, which may help you to anchor your focus.

Of course, we can't focus solely on design. Organization is important in creating a focus-friendly environment, too. You want a space where everything you need is within arm's reach. Thinking about your desk space still, you'll want to designate clear spaces for your essentials so that you're not constantly searching for a pen or your phone charger. Streamlining your workflow will make a significant difference as well. Consider how you can arrange your workspace to minimize unnecessary movement and decision-making. Maybe it's by placing your most used items on your dominant side, or perhaps it's by setting up a charging station near your desk. They're only small adjustments, but they can help you streamline your tasks and reduce your mental load, which will allow you to focus on what actually matters rather than logistical distractions.

You'll also need to set both physical and psychological boundaries. Designate specific areas for work and relaxation to signal to your brain when it's time to concentrate and when it's time to unwind. All too often, I'd bring my laptop to the sofa, and both my productivity and my ability to relax would suffer. If you share your home with other people, you might want to use visual cues like a closed door or a "Do Not Disturb" sign to communicate your focus time to other members of the household. This isn't just to set expectations with them; it will also reinforce your own commitment to maintaining a distraction-free environment. Boundaries help create a ritual of focus, where entering your workspace means stepping into a mindset of productivity and leaving it signals that it's time to transition into rest and personal time.

Reflection Time! Sensory Preferences

You may not have thought much about your sensory preferences and how they affect your focus before. If that's the case, try reflecting on your answers to these simple questions to help you understand what parts of your environment help or hinder your concentration.

- What colors make you feel calm?
- What sounds help you focus?
- What textures make you feel less distracted and more productive?

Use your answers to help you make small changes that align your space with your needs.

USING STIMMING AS A TOOL

If you're someone who needs to stim to help you manage your energy or self-soothe, this could help you to find your focus and calm when you're finding it difficult to concentrate. Stimming refers to repetitive movements or sounds that many of us with ADHD use to help us manage our emotions and self-regulate. It's a natural mechanism that can help you navigate overwhelming situations, and there's a high chance that you have already done it. Whether it's tapping your fingers to a silent beat or quietly humming a tune, these actions are grounding, and they provide comfort and stability. For many of us, stimming is a way to release built-up energy or handle sensory overload, but we can also use it as a productivity tool.

First, you need to identify the stimming activities that aid your concentration. Perhaps the rhythmic click of a pen or the tactile sensation of a stress ball keeps your mind centered. Mine is a little less conventional. I'm a very tactile person, and something that I find soothing is having a small bowl of uncooked rice on my desk. I run my fingers through it when I need to concentrate or I'm feeling stressed, and it helps me a lot. You could also integrate stimming breaks into organizational projects to refresh your mind and make it easier to tackle the next phase of your work with renewed concentration.

A lot of us do our best to fit our stimming into whatever environment we're in, but it's also possible to keep your needs in mind from the beginning, creating an environment that will accommodate them to improve your productivity. You could keep stimming tools like fidget spinners or tactile objects within easy reach on your desk so that you can use them easily when you need a moment of grounding. If you work outside of the home, there's no reason you couldn't still do this. If there's a quiet corner of your office where you can take stimming breaks without interruption or judgment, this could really help you to focus while at work.

I know that balancing stimming with social norms can sometimes be challenging, especially in professional or shared environments, but I don't believe we should carry any shame around this, and more often than not, when I've explained it to other people, I've been met with understanding and support. Don't be afraid to let your friends, family members, and colleagues know that you do this to help you self-regulate. Of course, it's also important to be careful that you're stimming at appropriate times and in appropriate places, but that doesn't mean that there aren't backup options. If you're in a meeting, you could try subtle stimming behaviors like toe-tapping or doodling, which may satisfy the need for sensory input without attracting attention. It's definitely not always appropriate for me to have a bowlful of rice in every situation, but what I can do is keep a soft piece of fabric in my pocket, which gives me the tactile stimulation I need when I have to be more subtle. This is an example of adapting to your environment in a way that respects both your needs and the social context at a time when you can't adapt the environment to meet *your* needs.

Many of us keep our stimming quiet, but it can be used as a tool to support our productivity and well-being, and it certainly isn't something to be ashamed of. The secret is to create an environment and lifestyle that honors your rhythms and needs, and this will offer you a path to greater focus and emotional balance.

TECH TOOLS TO ENHANCE FOCUS

We have advantages in the digital world that we wouldn't have been able to benefit from in the past, and technology can transform the way you manage tasks and maintain your focus. I've mentioned both Todoist and Trello before, but I'm bringing them up again because task management apps like these are so helpful for organizing your thoughts and priorities in a structured way. Todoist lets you break down tasks into subtasks, set deadlines, and assign priorities, all of which can be visually tracked with color-coded labels. Trello offers a more visual approach with its board and card system, and you can see all of your tasks at a glance. I use these apps to help me stay organized, but the real benefit I've felt is the reduced mental load of trying to remember everything at once, and this means that I can save my cognitive resources to concentrate on the task at hand—plus, I'm a lot less stressed.

There will always be those moments, though, when distractions seem to multiply, and focus-enhancing browsers like Cold Turkey can help with this. Cold Turkey locks you out of distracting websites so that you can work uninterrupted. I use it to block out social media, news sites, and a number of online rabbit holes that tend to derail my concentration. If you don't want to block them entirely, browser extensions like StayFocusd can limit the amount of time you spend on distracting websites. You set the rules and decide how much time is acceptable before the extension blocks access for the rest of the day. There's also the Forest app, which is designed to help you focus by growing a virtual tree that dies if you leave the app to check social media or messages. I respond well to games and visuals, so I love this one, and it really does work. I never want that tree to die! Tools like these create a sense of accountability at the same time as turning focus into a rewarding game rather than a chore.

We've talked a little about time management tools already, but I want to come back to them because they're so helpful for structuring your day. Apps that allow for time-blocking, such as Google Calendar, make it easy for you to dedicate specific time slots to different activities and see them depicted visually. A list of endless tasks is overwhelming for many of us with ADHD, but this breaks the day into manageable intervals and makes it seem less intimidating. You could also try digital timers like Timer+, which give you auditory reminders when it's time to switch tasks so that you stay on track and keep a steady workflow going.

The secret to making any digital tool work for you is to understand yourself and customize your tech solutions to fit your personal needs. A good place to start is to set personalized notifications and reminders that align with your daily routine and tell you when to start or stop a task. It's also a good idea to integrate calendar apps with other productivity tools in order to streamline your workflow. You can sync Todoist with your Google Calendar so that all your tasks and appointments are in one place, and you don't have to juggle multiple platforms or spend a lot of time managing the tools.

MANAGING TIME BLINDNESS

We talked about time blindness earlier in the book, and it's a struggle that many people with ADHD face daily. It's not that we lose track of time; we have a genuinely hard time perceiving its passage. There have been so many times that I've started a task only to look up and realize that hours have flown by without me noticing, and this has made me late and miss deadlines more times than I care to remember. If you also struggle with time blindness, you'll know that it can affect every aspect of planning and productivity, and it's hard to know how long any given task will take. You might find yourself consistently underestimating the amount of time you need, even for simple activities, and this can lead to a cascade of stress and missed opportunities. Once this has happened a couple of times in the day, you probably find yourself firmly stuck in a cycle of frustration, struggling to keep up with the demands of your day.

For me, improving time awareness has meant adopting strategies that ground me in the present. It almost seems too simple to suggest visual timers and clocks, but these weren't always a consistent part of my daily routine, and it made such a big difference when I started using them. Try placing a large clock in your workspace or using a timer app on your phone so that you have constant visual reminders of the time passing. They're such simple tools, but they can help you check in with reality and see a tangible representation of time that your mind might not naturally perceive on its own. It can also make a big difference to schedule regular time checks. Set alarms at intervals throughout your day to pause and assess your progress, which has the added benefit of giving you a moment to recalibrate your focus and adjust your schedule if you need to.

The key to building your time awareness is intention. Start by integrating time markers into your morning and evening routines. In the morning, you can use regular routines like breakfast or a morning walk as natural indicators that it's time to transition from one activity to the next. In the evening, you can aim to wind down activities at set times, perhaps by turning off screens half an hour before bed. Again, it's simple, but it will help you to establish a rhythm for your day. Regularly update and review your schedule so you can adjust your plans based on priorities and unforeseen changes. I have no doubt that this will simultaneously help you to manage your time and reduce your anxiety.

Tools and resources for managing time effectively are more accessible than ever now. Digital planners with built-in time-tracking features are widely available, and they offer a structured way to organize tasks and see the patterns in how you spend your time. Many of them include analytics that show patterns in your productivity, and this is really helpful if you want to make informed adjustments.

Time blindness is a real problem for many of us, and it will help a lot if you can build a framework that supports your needs and compensates for the challenges of ADHD so that you interact with time differently. I feel like I've had more control over my day since I improved my time awareness, and it's made such a difference in my ability to achieve my goals.

BATTLING ADHD PARALYSIS

Have you ever had one of those moments when your to-do list feels like a mountain, and you can't find a way to start climbing it? This is ADHD paralysis, and it often sneaks up on you and makes you freeze in the face of mounting tasks. You might be unable to make a decision, you might avoid tasks, or you might procrastinate, and to overcome it, you're going to need to be able to recognize the things that trigger this paralysis. Often, the culprit is an overwhelming task list without clear priorities, which means that every item seems equally urgent and important. When everything demands your attention, deciding where to begin becomes paralyzing. This can be even worse if you have a high-pressure deadline, which can exacerbate the problem and fill you with a sense of dread that stalls your action even further. It's the weight of expectation and the fear of not meeting it that can stop you in your tracks, and this, ironically, leaves you in a state of inaction.

You can overcome this, but you're going to need strategies for breaking tasks into smaller, more manageable pieces. Start by identifying the simplest part of the task—something so easy it almost feels trivial—just like me cleaning up my hallway rather than tackling the whole house. It might mean organizing a single drawer instead of the entire office or writing the first sentence of a report. They may be small things, but if you can break your tasks into actionable steps, you'll reduce the sense of overwhelm and point yourself in a forward direction. Setting micro-deadlines can also help, by which I mean short, specific deadlines that create a sense of urgency without the pressure of the final due date looming over you. It could be as small as devoting the next 20 minutes to a specific task, which will give you focus and encourage momentum.

Building momentum with small actions is key to breaking through paralysis. Begin with tasks that are easy and offer a quick win. The "two-minute rule" is an effective tool here. If a task takes less than two minutes to complete, do it immediately. It could be something as simple as answering an email, tidying a workspace, or making a short phone call. These small victories will give you the mental space you need to focus on the bigger tasks, as well as build your confidence and give you a sense of accomplishment (which will also motivate you to tackle larger tasks). Each completed task, no matter how minor, will reinforce your belief in your ability to take action and move forward.

Collaborating with peers is also helpful. It comes with mutual encouragement and shared motivation, which always makes any task feel less daunting. When you work alongside someone else, you create a shared momentum that can propel you both forward. It could be a study group, a coworker, or a friend—anyone you can share your goals with. Your job may not always allow for it, but group work sessions are great when you have the opportunity because they give you structured time and space to focus on tasks together. The collective energy of a group can be infectious, and I've certainly found that the problems I have with motivation when I'm on my own disappear completely in these situations.

Small steps lead to significant change, and this is just as true with ADHD paralysis and time blindness as it is with organizing your living space. The best part is that these strategies don't just help you get things done; they help you reclaim control over your tasks and, ultimately, your life. This is only one piece of the puzzle, though, and your emotional regulation also plays a significant role in your ability to stay focused and get organized. This is what we'll look at in the next chapter.

6

EMOTIONAL REGULATION AND ITS IMPACT ON ORGANIZATION

The path to lasting organization isn't paved with perfect systems - it's built on understanding the beautiful dance between your emotions and your environment. Let's learn these steps together.

If you've ever woken up feeling optimistic and ready to tackle the day, and then a small inconvenience has suddenly ignited an intense emotional response that derails your plans, you know a little something about emotional dysregulation. Your heart races, and suddenly, the tasks you had lined up seem like insurmountable challenges, even though you'd felt fully equipped to deal with them just moments before. Emotional dysregulation is a common symptom of ADHD, affecting between 30% and 70% of adults who live with it. It means you have difficulty managing your emotions, and this often leads to feelings that are more intense than the situation warrants. It manifests differently in different people. For me, it presents as anxiety; for you, it could be anger or frustration. However you experience it, it can be very difficult to regain control once it's surfaced, but don't worry. This is something you can overcome.

UNDERSTANDING EMOTIONAL DYSREGULATION

Emotional dysregulation has to do with the way the different parts of the brain work with each other, particularly the amygdala and prefrontal cortex, which function differently in people with ADHD. This can lead to unpredictable emotional responses, which can impact your decision-making and daily interactions. You might find yourself facing frequent mood swings that affect your ability to make clear, rational decisions, for example. The problem isn't just the emotional intensity, but also the challenge of calming down once your emotions have flared, which can leave you feeling exhausted and overwhelmed, and this can throw you into a cycle that affects your overall well-being and productivity.

The first step toward regulating your emotions is to recognize the triggers and patterns in your emotional responses. For many people, high-stress environments act as catalysts and exacerbate emotional dysregulation. You might notice that certain situations, like tight deadlines or interpersonal conflicts, trigger a stronger emotional reaction—they certainly cause my anxiety to flair. If you can understand your patterns, you have more chances to anticipate and prepare for them. For example, if a particular person or situation tends to provoke stress, you can develop strategies in advance to help you manage your response. Unfortunately, this means you can't just avoid your triggers: You have to experience them in order to identify them; only then can you empower yourself to approach them with a clearer mindset.

The impact of emotional dysregulation on organization and productivity is significant. When emotions run high, procrastination can become a default coping mechanism, and I know this all too well. The tasks on your to-do list might feel overwhelming, which may make you turn to avoidance as a way to manage the emotional overload. This tendency can result in disorganized thinking, and your scattered thoughts may make it difficult to prioritize and execute tasks. What you end up with is a mental fog, which reduces your ability to focus and manage your time effectively. The result is often a cluttered environment, both physically and mentally, where tasks pile up, and you're missing deadlines left, right, and center.

STRATEGIES FOR MANAGING RSD

Another challenge often faced by people with ADHD is Rejection Sensitivity Dysphoria (RSD). This emotional phenomenon can deeply impact individuals with ADHD, affecting their self-esteem, relationships, and overall mental well-being. It plays a significant role in emotional regulation, and it can influence your ability to stay organized and productive.

RSD is characterized by an intense emotional response to the perception of rejection or criticism, even when it may not be intended or is relatively minor. For those with ADHD, this sensitivity can amplify feelings of inadequacy, fear, and anxiety, and this, in turn, makes it challenging to engage fully in tasks. The overwhelming emotions triggered by RSD can lead to avoidance behaviors like procrastination, neglecting responsibilities, or withdrawal from social interactions, and this can make problems associated with organization and productivity even worse.

I've struggled with RSD myself, and it means that when I'm faced with criticism or the fear of rejection, I feel more vulnerable and anxious. For other people, the emotional turmoil can manifest as feelings of sadness, despair, or anger, all of which can derail focus and motivation. There's often a strong need for perfection (this is definitely true of me), but the fear of not measuring up can result in paralysis, leading to disorganization and uncompleted tasks. It's a cycle, and it can throw hurdles into your ability to maintain a structured and efficient approach to your daily responsibilities.

To overcome the effects of RSD, you'll need self-compassion and emotional regulation strategies. You have to acknowledge your feelings and recognize that RSD is a legitimate experience and that your feelings of rejection are valid. Allowing yourself to feel without judgment is important. These emotions are tied to your ADHD; they have nothing to do with your worth, and in order to recognize this, you have to be able to acknowledge your feelings in the first place.

This is just the first step, though. You'll also need to develop coping strategies, and these will vary from person to person. Good options are mindfulness, deep breathing exercises, and journaling, which can provide an outlet for processing your emotions and help reduce the intensity of RSD reactions. Building a support system will help, too. Engage in conversations with trusted friends, family, or support groups so that you can share your feelings and receive validation, which will help you to feel safe and accepted, whatever other feelings your RSD may be prompting.

Be realistic in your expectations of yourself. Remind yourself that imperfections are human, aim to set achievable goals, and allow yourself to make mistakes without dwelling on them. You want your focus to be on progress rather than perfection in order to alleviate the pressures that amplify RSD—otherwise, you're just feeding your fear. You can also use cognitive reframing techniques to reshape the way you interpret criticism or rejection. This is really about changing the way you look at these things. Instead of viewing feedback as a personal failure, try to see it as an opportunity for growth. Practice self-affirmation and remind yourself of your strengths and achievements to counterbalance negative self-talk.

Creating structured routines can also help you to manage the impact of RSD. Implementing the organization strategies we've talked about (like task lists, reminders, and scheduled breaks) will give you structure and reduce your feelings of overwhelm, and this will decrease the likelihood of experiencing RSD in response to perceived expectations. If you find that these strategies aren't working, or if RSD significantly impacts your daily life, it may be time to look for professional support. Working with a therapist or counselor who specializes in ADHD will give you access to tailored strategies that will help you navigate your emotional responses and develop healthier coping mechanisms.

MINDFULNESS TECHNIQUES FOR EMOTIONAL CONTROL

Mindfulness is the practice of being present and fully engaged in the current moment without judgment. When you have ADHD and often experience a whirlwind of thoughts, this can be very helpful. Mindfulness has been shown to reduce stress, improve focus, and enhance emotional regulation, and it gives you a greater sense of calm and balance, allowing you to respond to situations thoughtfully rather than reactively.

When I first heard about mindfulness, I assumed it would involve hours of meditation or complex rituals, and I couldn't see how I would find the focus or motivation to practice it. Thankfully, I was wrong. You can easily build simple practices into your routine to help you manage your emotions more effectively, one of the easiest being deep breathing exercises. Close your eyes and inhale slowly through your nose, holding your breath for a moment before exhaling gently. This will calm your mind, reduce your anxiety, and give you a greater sense of control.

You could also try body scan meditation, which will increase your awareness of the physical sensations in your body, helping you to release stress. To do this, find a quiet space and mentally scan your body from head to toe, noting any tension or sensations without judgment.

Mindful journaling may help, too. Set aside a few minutes each day to write about your emotions and experiences. This will help you to process your feelings constructively, and it will tell you a lot about your emotional landscape.

But practicing mindfulness doesn't even have to be as structured as this. It isn't about emptying the mind or achieving a state of perfect calm; it's about noticing your thoughts and emotions without getting swept away by them, and this can be done while you're doing other simple activities like walking, eating, or brushing your teeth. Natural moments like this will give you the opportunity to practice presence, gradually building mindfulness into your daily life.

Interestingly enough, mindfulness can also improve your organizational skills and focus. Before you dive into your to-do list each day, take a moment to center yourself and plan your schedule. Visualize your day, and prioritize your tasks based on their importance rather than their urgency. It may seem counterintuitive at first, but it will reduce the emotional bias that can cloud your judgment and make sure that you focus on what's really important. If you can integrate mindfulness into your organizational practices, you'll create a more intentional and thoughtful approach to managing your responsibilities, and this will only help your organizational skills.

Consistency in mindfulness practice is important, but this can be challenging, especially when you have ADHD. The mind naturally wanders, and you may get frustrated when your focus slips. Try not to judge yourself for this or let it put you off; instead, gently guide your attention back to the present moment. It's a skill that improves with practice and patience, I promise. For me, making it a habit was the thing that ensured I was consistent, and to do this, I created reminders to incorporate mindfulness into each day. I used a reminder on my phone, but you could use alarms or sticky notes—whatever works best for you.

Mindfulness Check-In

Set a daily reminder for a mindfulness check-in. When the alert goes off, pause for a moment, take a deep breath, and take in your surroundings. What do you hear, see, and feel? It's a simple exercise, but you can use it to anchor yourself in the present, and this will bring a sense of calm and awareness into the rest of your day.

COGNITIVE RESTRUCTURING FOR EMOTIONAL BALANCE

Cognitive restructuring is a powerful technique that can reshape how you perceive and respond to the world. It sounds complicated, but it's really just about changing the automatic thoughts that often run unchecked in your mind. These are often negative or irrational, and they act like background noise, influencing your emotions and actions without you even noticing. Perhaps you find yourself thinking, "I'll never get this done," or "I'm not good enough," and thoughts like this can easily become barriers, blocking your progress and fueling your anxiety. Cognitive restructuring invites you to challenge these thoughts, question their validity, and replace them with more balanced, rational alternatives. I like to think of it as rewiring the circuits in my mind.

To do this, you're going to work through a series of deliberate steps, each designed to break down and rebuild your thought patterns. The first is to recognize what those automatic negative thoughts are, which requires self-awareness and a willingness to pause and listen to your inner dialogue. Once you've done this, you can start to question these thoughts. Are they based on facts, or are they distortions shaped by fear or past experiences? What evidence do you have to support them? If you examine the proof, you can begin to dismantle the false narratives, which you can then replace with balanced alternatives. For instance, instead of "I'll never finish this project," you might say, "I can tackle this project step by step." All you're doing is shifting your language, but this is enough to change your mindset and make you more aware of other possibilities and solutions.

Cognitive restructuring is a valuable tool for managing your emotions and enhancing your productivity. As we've discussed, anxiety about completing tasks can paralyze you, but if you apply these cognitive restructuring techniques, you can reduce your anxiety, breaking the task into smaller, manageable parts and reframing your approach. This clarity in thinking often leads to better decision-making because it enables you to prioritize tasks, allocate your time effectively, and filter out the false beliefs that hold you back. When you clear away the fog of negative thoughts, you'll naturally create space for rational, focused action—and this can turn a cluttered desk or a daunting to-do list into a series of achievable goals.

Documenting your thoughts will help you to restructure your thought patterns. It will give you a structured way to track and analyze your thoughts. Write down each thought you want to challenge, the situation that triggered it, and your emotional response, and over time, you'll start to see recurring patterns and themes. Awareness is always the first step toward change, and this is no exception.

TRAINING YOURSELF IN COGNITIVE FLEXIBILITY

Wouldn't it be nice to be met with a sudden change in plans and be able to adapt with ease? You can! This is the power of cognitive flexibility, and it's something that can be quite difficult for those of us with ADHD, but it's a skill we can build. It's the mental agility that allows you to shift your thinking and adapt to new situations, a skill that's very helpful when life throws unexpected curveballs your way. Cognitive flexibility enhances your problem-solving abilities and fuels creativity, which will help you see challenges from multiple angles and come up with innovative solutions. The result of this will be that you're not confined to a single way of thinking, and this will make you more resilient when you come up against uncertainty.

Developing your cognitive flexibility can significantly improve your performance and encourage your creativity, especially when you're organizing spaces or tackling new projects. It allows you to draw upon diverse perspectives, which will give you a wealth of ideas that might not have surfaced with a more rigid approach. You'll be able to think outside the box, connect dots that seem to be unrelated, and find unique solutions to problems. In rapidly changing environments, cognitive flexibility is what allows you to pivot quickly and adjust your strategies as you need to without losing momentum. For example, if a project at work changes direction, your ability to adapt is what will keep you effective and help you find new paths to achieve your goals.

To develop your cognitive flexibility, engage in activities that challenge your usual thinking patterns. You might try puzzles, learn a new skill, or engage in discussions that push you to consider different viewpoints. These activities stimulate your brain, encouraging it to explore new pathways and enhancing your mental agility. Mindfulness practices can also train you to become more adaptable. They teach you to stay present, manage your stress, and approach problems with a calm and open mind, and this will allow you to respond thoughtfully rather than reacting impulsively, which is likely to make you better at making decisions and regulating your emotions.

This doesn't just relate to your professional life. Cognitive flexibility will also help you with organization and clean-up projects. If you've planned a major decluttering session only to find that your initial strategy isn't working, you can adjust your plan. Cognitive flexibility will allow you to consider multiple solutions to a single problem and find the one that fits the context best. The task will then become much more manageable *and* much more enjoyable because you'll be experimenting with different approaches and figuring out what works best for you. This is a powerful tool for building your resilience.

BUILDING RESILIENCE IN DAILY LIFE

Resilience is your ability to recover from setbacks, adapt to changes, and keep moving forward even when the path gets rough. It's not about never falling down; it's about how quickly you can get back up, and it's so important when you're managing ADHD because life is full of unexpected twists and turns. Every challenge you face—whether it's a missed deadline, an overwhelming task, or emotional upheaval—requires you to have a resilient mindset that will allow you to view obstacles as opportunities to learn and grow. Cultivating your resilience will help you develop the adaptability you need to thrive in a world that often demands flexibility and quick thinking.

Building resilience might sound like a daunting undertaking, but like everything else, it begins with a small step: setting realistic expectations and goals. It's easy to feel discouraged when your ambitions don't align with your reality, but if you set achievable goals, you'll set the stage for a series of small wins that will build both your momentum and your confidence. It's important, too, to have supportive people around you, people who understand the challenges you face and cheer you on. Their encouragement will be a powerful motivator, and they'll be there to give you the emotional support you need in order to persevere when things get tough.

To incorporate resilience into your organizational practices, you'll need to make a conscious effort to see setbacks as learning opportunities. When something doesn't go to plan, instead of seeing it as a failure, view it as a chance to learn what doesn't work. As you train yourself in this, you'll gradually be able to shift your focus from what went wrong to what can be improved, finding the silver lining in each setback and using it as fuel to refine your approach. You'll also need to be flexible when it comes to task management. Life is unpredictable, and plans often change, so it's important to be able to adjust your strategies in response to new information or circumstances. When someone pointed this out to me in relation to resilience, it was hard for me to see how it related, but as I focused on improving my flexibility, I realized that this is a key part of resilience. Challenges and changes used to stop me in my tracks and prevent me from making progress, but as I learned to become more flexible, I found that I was able to make progress, no matter what setbacks arose.

Let's look at an example of resilience in action. Someone working on a complex project might face numerous obstacles—tight deadlines, team disagreements, or unexpected technical issues, for instance. Instead of giving up, they persevere, breaking the project into smaller tasks and tackling each one with determination. This perseverance is a clear example of resilience. Maintaining a focus when emotions run high requires resilience, too. Distractions are inevitable, but resilient people develop strategies to keep their attention on the task at hand, even when they're feeling emotional. They might use techniques like time-blocking or setting clear boundaries to create an environment conducive to concentration. You might notice at this point that these are all strategies we've already discussed, so as long as you're using them, you're already building up your resilience.

Resilience plays a huge role both in managing ADHD and maintaining organization. It's what will allow you to persevere through difficulties, maintain your focus, and thrive in both your personal and professional pursuits. As we move on, we'll explore how the principles of resilience and organization can be applied to create structured programs and routines that will help you even more.

MAKE A DIFFERENCE WITH YOUR REVIEW

"The greatest gift you can give someone is the tools to help themselves."

— TEMPLE GRANDIN

Remember that feeling when you first realized your brain might work a little differently? When piles of stuff seemed to multiply overnight, and staying organized felt like trying to catch clouds? I've been there too. Some days, just finding matching socks felt like winning the lottery!

But here's the amazing thing - you're reading this because you took a chance on making changes. You decided to try something new, and that takes courage! Now, could you help someone else find their way too?

You see, lots of folks with ADHD are out there right now, feeling overwhelmed and alone. It takes just a tiny moment of your time, but your words could help…

- one more parent feel less guilty about their messy home
- one more student find ways to keep track of their stuff
- one more adult understand they're not lazy or broken
- one more person discover their path to organization
- one more ADHD brain find peace in the chaos

To share your experience and light the way for others, just scan this QR code to leave a review:

Thank you for being part of this journey! Together, we're building a community where everyone can find their way from chaos to calm.

With gratitude and hope,

Visionary Press

7

TASK INITIATION AND COMPLETION TECHNIQUES

Your ADHD brain doesn't lack motivation - it craves engagement. That same energy that makes starting feel impossible can become your greatest ally in finishing what matters most.

Let me tell you about one of the challenges I faced when I started writing this book. It was a project that I'd had on my agenda for weeks, but despite my intentions (and the strategies I was already well-versed in using), I sat in front of the screen, paralyzed. I rearranged my desk a thousand times; I scrolled aimlessly through social media; I even decided it was a great time to clean the windows! That first day, two hours had passed before I did anything to do with writing this book. I know that this is a common experience for people with ADHD. I call it the procrastination monster, and it calls to me all the time. I know what to do to combat it, but even still, it's a challenge I have to overcome on a regular basis (and that's where resilience comes into play).

OVERCOMING PROCRASTINATION

Procrastination in ADHD is not simply a matter of laziness or a lack of discipline, so stop beating yourself up about that. It's rooted in deeper psychological factors that can be addressed when you have the right strategies at your disposal.

For a lot of people, procrastination stems from a fear of failure and an overarching desire for perfection. The thought of starting a task and not meeting expectations can be paralyzing—and that's exactly how it was for me when I was faced with a blank page. In fact, it was compounded by a hefty dose of imposter syndrome in my case —how could I write a book about organization with ADHD if I couldn't even beat my own procrastination monster? I've also had projects in the past where my fear has been intertwined with a lack of motivation or interest, especially when the task didn't provide immediate gratification or engagement. ADHD can amplify these feelings, and as you may know all too well, this can make mundane or complex tasks seem even more daunting. Anxiety about task complexity complicates the matter even further. When a job seems complicated, we tend to see it as a huge mountain rather than a series of small hills, and this makes it difficult to take the first step. The result? A cycle of avoidance and stress, where the more you delay, the more overwhelming the task becomes.

We've talked about a lot of the things that will help you here already, and as you become better at them, you'll find it easier to overcome procrastination. The main thing I want to come back to is setting small, clear, achievable goals to give you focus and direction. Instead of an abstract idea like "finish the report," you want to break it down into tangible steps: "research topic," "outline sections," and "draft introduction." Now, you have a series of manageable actions instead of one daunting task.

This isn't the only strategy you have at your disposal, though. I've found visualization techniques to be very helpful, too—in fact, that was one of the things that helped me finally get started on this book. I spent a few minutes imagining that I'd already finished it and feeling the sense of relief and accomplishment it would bring. This boosted my motivation and reminded me of the benefits of completing the task, which helped me to see the path forward. The important thing about visualization is that you really see and feel yourself moving through each step of the process and achieving your desired outcome. This is because what you're doing here is priming your brain to effectively reach the goal, and in order to do this, you need to activate the same parts of the brain that will be involved in the action.

Having someone to hold you accountable is also helpful. This can provide the external motivation you need to beat procrastination. I find that knowing someone else is aware of my commitments is surprisingly powerful in propelling me forward when my motivation wanes. Try sharing your intentions with a friend or a colleague; I'd be willing to bet that it will give you a sense of responsibility and a fresh perspective.

Building a personalized procrastination toolkit is an excellent way to prepare for moments of inertia. I actually have a list over my desk to remind me of all these things, so it really feels like a toolkit when I notice procrastination setting in and realize I have to take action. Start by creating "if-then" plans for predictable procrastination triggers. For example, "If I start to feel overwhelmed, then I will take a five-minute break and reassess." This will help you to anticipate obstacles and have a plan ready to combat them. Incorporating the "two-minute rule" can also help here: Remember, if a task can be completed in two minutes or less, do it immediately.

Again, mindfulness practices can help. Mindful breathing exercises, where you focus on each breath, will reduce your anxiety and bring clarity to your thoughts. It will ground you in the present moment, and this will help you to focus your mind so that you can concentrate.

Reflection Time! Procrastination Patterns

Consider your last three instances of procrastination. Reflect on these questions:

- What was the task, and how did you feel about it?
- What triggered the procrastination?
- How did you eventually overcome it, or what prevented you from doing so?

Write your thoughts down in a journal. This self-reflection will help you identify patterns and develop personalized strategies to tackle procrastination more effectively in the future.

REWARD SYSTEMS FOR MOTIVATION

Do you remember when you were a child saving up for something you really wanted, and each injection of pocket money felt like a stepping stone toward it? That's the power of a well-designed reward system. For people with ADHD, motivation often hinges on the brain's dopamine-driven reward system. Dopamine, a neurotransmitter, plays an integral role in how you experience pleasure and satisfaction. When you accomplish something, your dopamine levels rise, and this reinforces the behavior and encourages you to repeat it. In ADHD, dopamine levels are often lower, making it harder to feel motivated by tasks that aren't immediately gratifying.

The first step in getting around this is understanding the difference between intrinsic and extrinsic rewards. Intrinsic rewards are internal feelings of satisfaction and accomplishment, while extrinsic rewards are tangible incentives like treats or leisure activities. For tasks that lack intrinsic appeal, a thoughtful reward system can provide the external push you need to get started and see the task through to the end.

To create a reward system that resonates with you, first, identify what you genuinely find rewarding. This is personal, and it varies greatly from one person to another. It could be as simple as taking a short break to read a book, indulging in a delicious snack, or watching an episode of your favorite show. What's important is that your rewards are meaningful to you. From here, you need to decide what the criteria are for earning those rewards. This could mean finishing a particular task or maintaining focus for a certain period of time. If you have a clear goal, you'll feel like the reward is well deserved, and it will also give you a sense of structure and direction. I actually find that the anticipation of a reward often transforms mundane tasks into something to look forward to, and it helps me to build a positive association with completing the task. Isn't it amazing how we can trick our brains that way?

You can easily incorporate rewards into your daily routine, even for minor tasks. They don't have to be extravagant rewards. Even small treats like a piece of chocolate or a walk in the fresh air can be enough to boost your motivation. That way, you can reserve larger rewards to help you achieve significant milestones. Perhaps you've been working toward a larger goal, like completing a major project or maintaining a streak of productivity. Celebrating these successes with a special outing or buying something you've wanted for ages will reinforce your hard work and dedication. I'm a big believer in including rewards in my daily life: It makes productivity a more enjoyable experience, and it prompts me to recognize my achievements.

All of this said, it's important to balance rewards with your responsibilities. Rewards are powerful motivators, but if you rely too heavily on them, they may undermine your intrinsic motivation. The goal is to use rewards as a tool to build habits and give you a sense of accomplishment, but they shouldn't be the sole reason for your actions. They should complement and enhance the natural satisfaction that comes from completing tasks and meeting goals, and as you become more accustomed to working toward rewards, you may find that the tasks themselves begin to carry their own intrinsic value, and you'll need those external incentives less.

Reward System Planner

Create a simple planner to track your tasks and the rewards you want to pair with them. Divide the page into sections: *Task*, *Reward*, *Criteria Met*, and *Reflection*. Use this to set and evaluate goals, noting what works and what needs adjustment. Reflect on how the rewards influence your motivation and productivity and make changes as you need to. This will help you to develop a reward system that's both effective and adaptable, and it will support your journey toward more consistent motivation and task completion.

TASK BREAKDOWN: FROM OVERWHELM TO ACTION

I know all too well that when you have a mountain of tasks in front of you, it can feel paralyzing, and your mind races just thinking about where to begin. For many adults with ADHD, the prospect of tackling a complex task is daunting, and this can lead to feelings of anxiety and avoidance. But, as we've already discussed, if you break tasks down into smaller, more manageable steps, each part becomes easier. It will also improve your clarity and reduce your anxiety around large projects.

Prioritizing tasks based on their urgency and importance will also help. Some tasks may need your immediate attention, while others can wait. You can use a priority matrix to help you decide what to tackle first, which will help you to focus your energy where it's needed the most. It sounds like a complex idea, but really, all a priority matrix asks you to do is rate your tasks according to their urgency and the amount of time they require so that you can see what you need to prioritize first. It may help you to have a visual aid here. Consider using flowcharts or mind maps to visually organize your tasks and sub-tasks so that you can see how each piece fits into the larger picture.

We often think of processes like this as being work-related, but you can apply them to any task. Take, for example, the project of decluttering your home office. The best way to approach this would be to set a clear goal: a functional, organized workspace, perhaps. Next, identify the major components involved in achieving that outcome, such as sorting papers, organizing supplies, and setting up a filing system. For each component, you can list the steps you'll need to take in order to complete it. Sorting papers might involve gathering all your loose documents, categorizing them, and filing or shredding them as necessary. When you lay out each step like this, you'll have a framework to guide your actions and keep you focused. You can do the same thing with organizing your kitchen, breaking it down into phases to make it more manageable. You might start by clearing the countertops, moving to the pantry, and finishing with the refrigerator.

Despite its benefits, task breakdown can present its own challenges. Sometimes, it leads to decision paralysis and indecision for me, and the sheer number of choices can stall me in a state of inaction. I've gotten around this by setting time limits for making a decision. Give yourself just a few minutes to decide on each step so that you don't get stuck. It's also important to ensure that task breakdown doesn't lead to over-complication. It's helpful to outline the steps, but don't get bogged down in unnecessary details. Keep the process simple and focused, checking that each step directly contributes to the overall goal. Ask yourself, "Is this step necessary, or am I overthinking it?" I ask myself this a lot, and very often, I *am* overthinking it and trying to give myself an unnecessary extra step.

MAINTAINING MOMENTUM IN TASK COMPLETION

When you have momentum, you feel like you're in the zone, ticking off tasks easily and efficiently. When you have ADHD and you spend so much time battling organization and productivity, when it happens it feels like a gift. The secret to maintaining it is consistent action. The more you do, the more you *can* do. Each task you complete fuels the next, and this creates a snowball effect where progress builds upon itself. What it comes down to is creating a rhythm that sustains your productivity over time.

Setting interim goals is a good way to do this. These smaller milestones act as checkpoints, allowing you to track your progress and stay motivated. Each time you reach an interim goal, take a moment to acknowledge your progress. This will reinforce your commitment and provide a morale boost that will encourage you to keep going. Positive self-talk will help to keep your spirits high when the going gets tough, so make an effort to acknowledge your wins and remind yourself of your capabilities and the reason you're putting in the effort.

No matter how well you plan, you're going to face interruptions and setbacks. It could be an unexpected phone call, a sudden change in plans, or simply a wandering mind, but it *will* happen. To keep momentum in these moments, you'll need contingency plans. If you know that a particular time of day is prone to interruptions, plan tasks that require less focus during that period. This way, you can reserve your most productive hours for tasks that demand your full attention. You'll also need strategies that will help you to recover from setbacks quickly. Instead of dwelling on what went wrong, focus on what you can do next. You might be moving at a slower pace than you were, but you're still moving forward.

To keep up the momentum in the long term, you'll need to review your goals regularly to make sure that they're still aligned with your needs and circumstances. This will allow you to adapt to changes, whether they're shifts in your work environment or evolving personal goals. It will also give you an opportunity to celebrate your achievements and recognize your progress. Try to keep a growth-oriented mindset so that you see each task and each challenge as an opportunity to learn and grow. It will shift your focus from getting things done to how you can do them better, and this will keep your momentum alive.

Let me take this opportunity to remind you that it's not about perfection. It's about progress. Every single step you take contributes to a larger picture of productivity and personal growth—and in the next chapter, we'll explore how leveraging your ADHD traits can boost your productivity even further.

8

LEVERAGING YOUR ADHD TRAITS FOR ENHANCED PRODUCTIVITY

Every trait that's ever been labeled as a challenge - your creativity, your sensitivity to the environment, your ability to hyperfocus - is actually a key to unlocking your most productive self. Let's turn those keys together.

When you live with ADHD, it's very easy to focus on the qualities that make life more difficult for you, but it does come with some traits that can be really useful. When you know how to harness these traits effectively, they can be very helpful in balancing the more difficult aspects of ADHD, and that's what I'd like to focus on in this chapter.

EMBRACING HYPERFOCUS AS A STRENGTH

On one side of the coin, we have procrastination, but on the other, we have hyperfocus, the phenomenon that can have us lost in a task for hours with very little awareness of what else might be going on around us. Hyperfocus is a state of intense concentration where distractions seem to vanish, allowing you to immerse yourself fully in whatever you're doing. We can use this as a productivity tool, but it can lead to unintended consequences if it's not managed properly. The secret is to know how to channel this intense focus so that it becomes an asset.

Hyperfocus is characterized by a deep absorption in a task, often triggered by activities that are particularly engaging or stimulating. This might occur while working on a project you're passionate about or during a hobby that captivates your interest. Unfortunately, it doesn't happen on command (trust me, I've tried!) It catches you unexpectedly, and in my experience, it often leads to a loss of awareness of time and my surroundings. This can result in neglecting other responsibilities or self-care, as hours can pass you by without you even noticing. How, then, can you harness its potential? The trick is to recognize the scenarios in which hyperfocus is likely to occur.

To channel hyperfocus productively, it's a good idea to set specific goals before you dive into focus-heavy activities. Identify the tasks you want to accomplish and break them down into clear, manageable objectives. This will give you a roadmap that will reduce the likelihood of you drifting into less productive areas. Be sure to schedule breaks to help you manage your energy levels and prevent burnout. I use a timer to remind myself to pause, stretch, or have a glass of water, and I find that this gives me a balance between intense focus and rest.

You can also create conditions that support beneficial hyperfocus. Minimize your distractions by setting up a workspace that encourages concentration, just as we talked about earlier in the book. This may mean silencing unnecessary notifications, organizing your desk to reduce clutter, or using noise-canceling headphones to block out background noise. Let other members of your household or office know that you're in focus mode. A sign on your door or a quick message to your colleagues should stop them from interrupting you so you can fully engage in your tasks.

You'll need to make a conscious effort to balance hyperfocus with your other responsibilities. Otherwise, you run the risk of your intense concentration overshadowing your broader obligations. Again, alarms and timers can help you here, prompting you to switch tasks at appropriate intervals. Let your family, friends, or coworkers know when you need to concentrate and when you'll be available, which will help everyone to manage their expectations, reduce the risk of misunderstandings, and give you a set time at which you need to come out of your focused state.

Reflection Time! Hyperfocus Self-Assessment

Take a moment to reflect on your experiences with hyperfocus. Consider the following questions:

- What tasks or activities most frequently trigger your hyperfocus?
- How does hyperfocus affect your awareness of time and surroundings?
- What steps can you take to create a focus-friendly environment?
- How can you communicate your hyperfocus needs to those around you?

Use your answers to develop a personal strategy that will allow you to use your hyperfocus effectively.

UNLEASHING THE POWER OF CREATIVITY

My greatest gift is my creativity, and I'd hazard a guess that it might be one of yours, too. When we have ADHD, our minds often move with remarkable speed and agility, which means we can make novel connections and generate ideas that others might miss. If we can channel this effectively, this creativity can be a huge help for organization, allowing us to come up with innovative solutions and approach challenges in new ways.

We don't always think of creativity as being compatible with structure and organization, but it can substantially enhance your organizational skills. Creativity is what allows you to approach organizational tasks from unique angles and brainstorm unconventional solutions to common challenges. You might find new ways to categorize and prioritize your tasks, for example, or you might come up with a personalized organizational system that caters to your needs better than a conventional approach would.

Embrace your creative instincts so that you can develop systems that resonate with you. Use color-coded schedules, mind maps, or custom planners; categorize items in a way that makes sense to you even if no one else would get it—let your imagination run free in creating tools and processes that suit your preferences and stimulate your interest. This is how you'll make organization more engaging, and that's going to make your approach more effective.

One thing I like to do is use images and stories to help my memory and recall. This is based on the Method of Loci, often referred to as "the memory palace," which works by associating a familiar setting with the information you want to recall. You choose a familiar setting (I usually use a room in my house, but it could be your town or a familiar street) and visualize yourself walking through the space. Then you start "placing" the things you need to remember in different places around that space; before visualizing yourself, going back around and picking up everything in the same order, you put it down. You can do it with anything. Most commonly, it's a technique I turn to when I'm thinking about what I need to put on a shopping list, but I can't get to a pen and paper yet. I might "place" milk by the lamp in the corner, bread on the sofa, apples on the window ledge, and tomatoes on the coffee table. Having the imagery in my mind really helps me to remember the items when I get around to making the list.

Your creativity can also be used for stress relief. Several studies have found that creative activities are helpful in reducing stress and anxiety, and activities like drawing, writing, or playing music are good outlets for self-expression and relaxation, clearing your mind and restoring your focus. What's more, creative thinking has been associated with greater adaptability, so channel your creativity when you're faced with change so you can swiftly adjust your plans and priorities as you need to.

Creativity can also play a significant role in group settings, and you can use yours to make team interactions more vibrant and dynamic. Your innovative ideas may inspire other people, and this can be a huge asset in collaboration. You can unleash your creativity to redefine the boundaries of what it means to be organized. This trait—often viewed through the lens of artistry and innovation—can really help with productivity. Your creative mind is something to be celebrated. It brings color and vigor to the structure of life, and this can be an asset in your quest to become more organized.

HYPERACTIVITY AS A SUPERPOWER

While it can be challenging to manage, you can choose to view your hyperactivity as an extraordinary superpower fueled by high energy and enthusiasm. The boundless energy you have can ignite excitement both within you and in those around you, and if you're able to channel it effectively, you can use it to turn mundane tasks into exciting and engaging missions.

Many of us worry that we need to tone down our hyperactive natures, but it allows us to bring a unique vibrancy to every project we're involved in and every interaction we have. Your enthusiasm can breathe life into organizing tasks that might otherwise seem monotonous or overwhelming. It's true that hyperactivity can be a distraction, but it can also be a great source of motivation and inspiration. Your ability to approach tasks with a sense of urgency and passion can turn working on a challenging project into an exhilarating experience, not just for you but for anyone lucky enough to join you.

But how do you actually channel hyperactivity effectively? For me, an effective way is to incorporate movement into my daily routines. Physical activity helps me to channel my enthusiasm constructively, and this helps me to stay engaged and focused. Studies conducted on children with ADHD confirm that this is a helpful approach. Try incorporating activities into your work sessions—whether it's dancing to your favorite playlist while sorting through papers, using a standing desk, or taking brisk breaks for a quick walk. Blending movement and productivity like this will keep your enthusiasm high, and if you have other people around you, it will also provide a contagious source of motivation for them.

Your natural exuberance makes you a captivating person to be around, and it may inspire those around you to tap into their own energy. Use your enthusiasm to rally your friends, family, or colleagues to turn collaborative tasks into lively group efforts. Your ability to infuse excitement into even the simplest tasks—like organizing a shared workspace or planning an event—will make the process feel collaborative and fun, and it will create a sense of camaraderie and motivation within the group.

Variety is important, too. If you engage in different activities, you'll keep your mind active and energized. If a task begins to feel monotonous, don't hesitate to shake things up! Experiment with new organizational systems, change your work environment, or invite others to join you in a different setting. You may even inspire those around you to innovate alongside you, and this will breed an atmosphere rich with creativity and enthusiasm.

By embracing hyperactivity as your superpower, you can redefine the notion of productivity, and I think this is especially important if your energy was viewed as a "problem" in your school days. Your high energy and enthusiasm fuel your journey and uplift those in your presence—and you're no longer required to sit still and listen to the same teacher all day. Your hyperactivity is a remarkable gift, and you can use it to make both organization and life in general more engaging and enjoyable for yourself and everyone around you.

As we move forward, we'll explore the environments and support systems that can help you maximize both this and the other traits we've looked at in this chapter for sustained success.

9

ROOM-SPECIFIC STRATEGIES FOR TARGETED ORGANIZATION

Every room tells a story of how we live, dream, and move through our days. Your ADHD mind doesn't need a Pinterest-perfect space - it needs rooms that understand and support the beautiful way your thoughts flow.

One of the biggest problems for me when it came to home organization was that I didn't realize that different rooms required different approaches. I was trying to view the whole house as one task, and I was trying to approach that task in a uniform way. I was fighting a losing battle, and it was only when I started thinking of each room as a separate entity that I was able to make any headway. In this chapter, we'll take the main spaces in your home and look at organizational strategies to use with each one.

CONQUER YOUR KITCHEN!

There was a time when I was constantly overwhelmed every time I walked into my kitchen. Pots and pans would be stacked haphazardly, spice jars were scattered across the counter, and I could never see past the clutter to find anything I needed. Sound familiar? Your kitchen should be a place of creativity and nourishment, but for many people with ADHD, it more often feels chaotic. If you organize this space strategically and make thoughtful adjustments to its layout, you can reclaim your kitchen and enjoy using it again.

Someone once told me to think of organizing my kitchen as creating little workstations and grouping things by task, and it completely changed the way I approached it. I now have a particular area for my morning routine, which has a coffee station that includes my coffee maker, mugs, coffee, sugar, and filters. There's a cleaning zone near the sink with dish soap, sponges, and towels all kept together. I also have a baking station, where mixing bowls, measuring cups, and baking sheets live, and a chopping station, where I keep all my cutting boards and knives. Having these zones has drastically reduced the amount of time and effort I spend searching for things, and it means I can move seamlessly from one task to the next. I also keep the items I use the most within easy reach. All the dishes and utensils that I use on a daily basis are now kept in easily accessible cabinets or drawers, and this means I'm not always reaching up or bending down, which I found interrupted my focus and flow. I love cooking, and I'm finally able to focus on the joy of it again rather than feeling constantly stressed out.

You have ADHD, and this means that you're going to need storage solutions that support the way your mind works. Labeling your shelves and containers is a good idea, and it will help you make sure that everything has a designated place to return items back to. Try using transparent containers for pantry items so that you can see their contents at a glance without rummaging. What surprised me when I did this was that it stopped me from over-purchasing, and this meant that I was naturally reducing the amount of clutter I was generating. Open shelving is a good idea, too. It will provide easy access and act as a visual reminder of what's available and what you need to replenish. If you keep the foods you use most often on these shelves, you'll have a system that naturally supports your organization, and this will help you to maintain order.

Try to audit your pantry and fridge on a regular basis so you can discard things that have expired and reorganize the shelves as you need to. This routine will keep your kitchen tidy and ensure that you're using fresh ingredients all the time. You have no idea how many very old half-used jars I used to accumulate before I started doing this!

Kitchen Layout Checklist

To support your kitchen transformation, create a checklist that outlines the steps for optimizing your layout. Include tasks like grouping items by task and setting up workflow zones. Use this checklist to guide your reorganization.

CREATING A PEACEFUL BEDROOM SANCTUARY

The world outside is noisy and chaotic, but in your bedroom, you should find refuge. This wasn't always the case for me, and the space wasn't conducive to helping me unwind when there were clothes scattered everywhere. You want to design your bedroom with calmness in mind so that it promotes relaxation and rest. Start by choosing soothing colors. Soft blues, gentle greens, or warm neutrals will help you to create a tranquil atmosphere. I have a lot of pale blue in my bedroom, and it calms my senses as soon as I walk into the room. Soft lighting is a good idea, too; perhaps a bedside lamp with a warm glow or fairy lights around the bedframe. You might even want to use calming scents like lavender or chamomile in the form of scented candles or essential oils. These scents can be really helpful if you have a hard time winding down because they signal to your brain that it's time to sleep.

You don't want clutter to interrupt the tranquility you've established, so keep your storage simple and effective. Visual clutter can quickly disrupt your sense of calm. You could use under-bed storage for seasonal items so that you have more space in your closet and keep the things you don't need out of sight. Drawer organizers are great for clothes and accessories; they'll make it easy for you to find what you need without having to rummage through piles. These are only small adjustments, but they can really help you build a visually clean space, and this will help you focus on rest. A clutter-free environment will soothe both your eyes and your mind, and you'll find it easier to wind down at night.

Clutter is a problem, but that doesn't mean that you can't personalize your bedroom; in fact, doing so will make it feel more like a sanctuary. Display meaningful art or photographs that bring you joy and comfort so that the space feels like it's truly yours and reflects your personality. You might even want to add plants for a touch of nature. They add a sense of vitality to the room while purifying the air. If you're not great with plants, you can still do this; just choose low-maintenance options like succulents or snake plants.

HOME OFFICE HARMONY

Your office should be a place of productivity, but very often, it's a minefield of distractions, and as you know, this isn't helpful if you have ADHD. However, there are ways you can turn your workspace into a haven of concentration. We talked about putting your desk in a place where it gets a lot of natural light, but it's also a good idea to position it away from high-traffic areas to minimize visual distractions. If you're working at home, there's a huge temptation to get caught up in household activities, and this is less likely to happen if you do this. Remember those noise-canceling headphones too!

You want a streamlined workspace, so organize your office supplies and documents carefully. You might consider implementing a filing system for important documents, if you don't have one already, categorizing them in a way that makes sense to you—such as by project or urgency. This will help you keep your space tidy, and it will mean you can quickly retrieve any document you need without a frantic search. Use caddies for pens, paper clips, and other small supplies. These can sit neatly on your desk so that you have everything you need on hand without cluttering your desk.

Home Office Setup Checklist

Create a checklist to optimize your home office setup. Include tasks like arranging your desk, setting up noise-canceling headphones, and organizing your supplies. This will help you to make sure that each element of your office is tailored to support your focus and efficiency.

LIVING ROOM LIBERATION!

The living room is the heart of your home. It's the place you entertain guests, it's the place you have meaningful conversations, and it's a place where you relax. For those of us with ADHD, managing a room that hosts such a variety of activities can sometimes feel overwhelming. Just like in the kitchen, defining functional zones that cater to the different purposes your living room serves can help with this. Perhaps you'll create a cozy reading nook with a comfortable chair and a warm lamp. Maybe you'll have an entertainment area with neatly organized media storage to keep games, movies, and remotes in check. You might have an area where you keep wine glasses and bottles for easy access when friends come over. It's easier to stop clutter from accumulating when you have zones like this, and you'll find it easier to transition between activities without losing track of items.

To keep your living room tidy and visually appealing, try using baskets for loose items like remote controls and magazines. They'll conceal the clutter while adding a decorative touch to the room. Floating shelves are an elegant storage option, too. I love these, and they mean I can display my ornaments and books without cluttering up the floor or coffee tables.

When it comes to adapting your living room to serve a variety of purposes, flexible furniture can be very helpful. Modular seating arrangements can be reconfigured to accommodate anything from a solo movie night to a family game session, and choosing something like this means that your space can evolve with your lifestyle and suit every occasion you need it to. Coffee tables with hidden storage compartments are helpful, too; they give you a place to tuck away board games, blankets, or other extraneous items that might otherwise clutter your space.

Creating a welcoming atmosphere is the final touch that brings a living room to life. Arrange your furniture to facilitate conversation, ensuring that seating is oriented towards each other rather than a screen. This will encourage interaction and connection, and your living room will become a place where people naturally gather. You can add throw pillows and blankets for a cozy touch, too. These small details will make the space feel comfortable, and they'll also allow you to express your personality.

BATHROOM BREAKTHROUGH!

Your bathroom is where you start and end your day, and even in a small area, every square inch can be optimized for efficiency and tranquility. Over-the-door storage solutions are a great way to introduce more space without the need for renovations. Hooks for towels, caddies for toiletries, and a hanging rack for bathrobes can turn your door into a storage solution. Corner shelving can add depth to your bathroom and make use of dead space for storing essentials like shampoo or soap. Tiered organizers can hold everything from towels to toiletries without overcrowding your counters. Magnetic strips on medicine cabinet doors can hold small metal items like tweezers or nail clippers, freeing up drawer space. It's all about thinking creatively again, and these small adjustments will help you to create an environment where everything is within reach without being cluttered. Better yet, your daily routine will become much easier to navigate.

You can make this even more effective by grouping items by use. You might keep all your skincare products together, separate from your haircare items, for example. This will minimize the morning scramble, as you won't need to search for that elusive moisturizer or hair gel. It might sound like an unnecessary step, but I also have a routine checklist on a small whiteboard in my bathroom. I know that I'm always in a rush in the morning, and I often forget things, so I have a list of everything I want to remember to do—even brushing my teeth goes on there! I like this structure. It brings me a sense of order and predictability, and I find it sets a positive tone for the rest of the day.

Hygiene is a must in the bathroom. Make sure you clear out expired products regularly to make sure that you're using fresh, effective products and not building up clutter. Clear containers are helpful for both cleanliness and accessibility. If you store cotton swabs, cotton balls, or other small items in transparent jars, you'll be able to see exactly what you have at a glance, and it will be easier to find what you need—plus, you'll know that everything's safe and hygienic.

Each space in your home plays a distinct role in your daily life, and thoughtful organization can help you build environments that support you as you manage your ADHD and enhance your lifestyle. In the next chapter, we'll explore how to develop structured programs and routines to make your organizational journey even more effective.

10

DEVELOPING STRUCTURED PROGRAMS AND ROUTINES

What if I told you that the right kind of structure could set your ADHD mind free? Not the rigid routines that feel like cages, but flexible frameworks that give your creativity room to soar while keeping you grounded.

Having an organized environment is one thing, but you're also going to need to have an organized lifestyle if you're going to get the most out of this and keep it functioning as you want it to. Let's look at the structures you can build into your life to help with this.

DESIGN YOUR OWN 30-DAY CHALLENGE

You might be itching to get started with your organization once you've finished reading this book, but the chances are that excitement will wear off quickly, and you'll find yourself staring at an endless to-do list. I know this because I've been in exactly the same position. The tasks seem insurmountable, and your motivation dwindles as the days pass. You're starting something new, and you need to be able to keep up the momentum to see it through. This is why committing to a 30-day challenge is a good idea. It will harness the power of repetition so that new habits can take root. The goal is to dedicate a month to focusing on a specific area so that you reinforce behaviors until they become second nature.

I thought about designing a 30-day program for you, but the problem with this is that it needs to be personal if it's going to cater to your needs. Instead, I'm going to ask you to design it yourself. Identify the areas that best match your personal goals right now. You might want to establish a morning routine, declutter your living space, or enhance your focus at work. Whatever your objective, tailor the challenge to fit those needs. Set clear and measurable outcomes for each day, such as, "Spend 15 minutes sorting email." Be sure to avoid vague intentions like "Be more organized" so that you can see a clear path forward.

To develop a daily plan for success, break down the challenge into manageable chunks, just as we talked about earlier in the book. Start by outlining a day-by-day schedule, incorporating progressive milestones that will allow you to track your progress. Each day should build upon the last to give you a sense of achievement and forward momentum. I'd recommend allocating specific time blocks for more challenging activities; that way, you're more likely to treat them as appointments you can't miss. You're also more likely to stay focused, and there's less likelihood of being derailed by distractions. Remember, you can always use visual aids like charts or planners to map out your journey. These are so helpful for me. As I mark off completed tasks, the satisfaction of progress fuels my determination to keep going.

Your 30-day challenge isn't set in stone. You can evaluate and adjust at any time; in fact, this is an essential part of the process. You need to be able to change anything that isn't working. Set aside time each week to review your progress, celebrate your successes, and identify areas that need adjusting.

Reflection Time! Focusing Your 30-Day Challenge

Take a moment to reflect on an area you'd like to improve. Consider these questions:

- What specific goal do you want to achieve in the next 30 days?
- How can you break this goal into daily, actionable steps?
- What tools or resources will support your progress?
- How will you evaluate and adjust your challenge to enhance its effectiveness?

Write your thoughts in a journal and use them to tailor the challenge to your needs. This will be far more effective than any cookie-cutter challenge I could give you.

DAILY ROUTINES FOR CONSISTENCY

Ideally, you want to start each day with a clear sense of purpose, knowing exactly what lies ahead, and this is something you can achieve if you build consistent daily routines. If you can establish predictable patterns, you'll be able to improve your productivity because you'll be wasting less mental energy on making decisions. When we know what's coming next, we can focus on the task at hand rather than getting bogged down in choices.

Building effective morning and evening routines is the secret to structuring your day. As we discussed in Chapter 2, mornings set the tone for the hours ahead, so begin with rituals that ground, energize, and prepare you. Whether it's a short meditation session, a brisk walk, or simply enjoying a quiet cup of coffee, the predictable rituals you engage in every morning will help your mind to transition from rest to action and ground you in the present moment. Your evening routine, meanwhile, is a chance to unwind and reflect. Wind-down activities like reading, journaling, or practicing gratitude will help ease you into relaxation mode and signal to your brain that it's time to rest. My evening always looks the same. I take a warm bath, I read for half an hour, and I write down what I'm grateful for. This gives me a sense of closure on the day and paves the way for a restful night's sleep, and it's a ritual I look forward to every day.

What you want to make sure of is that your daily routines become habitual rather than sporadic, so you want to include core activities that will support this. Regular exercise, for instance, apart from being good for your physical health, promotes mental clarity and emotional balance, and it can improve your focus, attention, and ability to make decisions. By scheduling it into your day, it will stop feeling like an obligation and become a rewarding part of your routine, and this will help it to become habitual.

Self-care practices should be an integral part of your routine, too. This might be meditation or stretching, it could be taking some time to read or listen to music, or you might carve out a moment for reflection or journaling. When you embed this time into your day, you'll create a rhythm that nurtures both your body and your mind.

No matter how good your intentions are, however, life is unpredictable, and you'll need to make sure that your routines are adaptable enough to accommodate this. You might have to take a business trip, or there could be a family emergency; it could simply be a shift in your daily schedule, but flexibility is going to be key to sustaining your routines. Come up with some contingency plans well before you need them, such as packing a travel kit with the things you need for your routine or identifying alternative activities for times when you can't do what you usually do. I go for a jog most mornings, but I hate going in the rain, so I have a backup plan for when the weather's not on my side. Change used to derail my progress, but having a backup plan allows me to adapt. After all, a routine should be a tool, not a chain. It's not meant to restrict your life; it's meant to support it.

Reflection Time! Evaluating Your Daily Routine

Take a moment to assess your current routine. Ask yourself:

- What activities are non-negotiable for your well-being and productivity?
- How can you structure your morning and evening routines to support these activities?
- Are there areas where flexibility is needed to accommodate potential changes?

Note your thoughts in a journal to help you build a routine that truly serves your needs.

ACCOUNTABILITY PARTNERS

It's daunting to go it alone when you're making significant changes in your life, and this is where accountability partners come into play. They can give you the motivation, support, and encouragement you need to stay on track. Your accountability partner is someone who can cheer you on and give you feedback and perspective on your progress. They'll see your blind spots, highlight your achievements, and help you overcome obstacles. Better yet, the shared experience will create a sense of camaraderie, and this will make challenges seem less intimidating and successes feel more rewarding.

You can't just pick anyone, though. It's important to find someone whose goals and values align with your own so that you're both committed to the process and both of you can thrive. Look for someone who shares your interests and has similar commitment levels. You'll need to be able to communicate openly with this person. An effective partner is someone you can talk to honestly, without fear of judgment. They need to be willing to listen and provide constructive feedback so that you maintain focus and motivation.

You want your collaboration to be as effective as possible, so set clear expectations and goals with your accountability partner from the beginning. Check in with each other regularly so you can review your progress and address any roadblocks. You can also set joint milestones together to keep you both accountable and sustain your commitment. For instance, if you're both working on establishing a morning routine, you might agree on specific activities and timelines. In my experience, knowing someone else is counting on me adds an extra layer of motivation and pushes me to persevere even when it gets tough.

You don't necessarily have to be in the same place as your accountability partner to make this work. You can use digital tools to communicate and keep track of your progress. You might use shared calendars to schedule check-ins and milestone reviews, or you might use apps like Trello or Google Sheets to track your progress. You can also have virtual calls and use messaging apps so that, even when life gets busy, you can keep up the connection and mutual support.

Reflection Time! Finding Your Accountability Partner

Reflect on the following questions to identify a suitable accountability partner:

- What are your personal goals and values, and do they align with those of anyone you know?
- How frequently would you like to check in with your partner, and what form should these meetings take?
- What qualities do you value in a partner (e.g., honesty, encouragement, or constructive feedback)?

Discuss these reflections with potential partners to make sure you pick the right person and establish a strong foundation for your collaboration from the beginning.

USING TECHNOLOGY TO SUPPORT YOUR ROUTINE

Technology is so helpful for managing routines. My smartphone is kind of like a personal assistant that reminds me of important tasks, schedules my day, and even automates repetitive chores. It's such a small device, but it contains so much! Digital planners and reminder systems will help you manage your time more efficiently by sending alerts for appointments, deadlines, and breaks. Automation tools can handle repetitive tasks, like sending out weekly reports or managing emails. Use these technologies. They'll give you a framework that supports your daily life, and this means that your energy can go into what actually matters to you.

Of course, for any of this to be effective, you'll need to choose the right applications and tools. When you're evaluating app features, consider which aspects of task management are most challenging for you. Do you struggle with prioritizing tasks, or is it remembering deadlines that trip you up? Look for apps that excel in these areas. Once you've made your choice, you'll want to customize the settings so that you're reminded of tasks gently rather than being startled into action. You might also need to set boundaries for tech use so that it doesn't become a distraction. Allocate specific times for checking emails or social media so that it doesn't encroach on your productive hours. Technology should complement your routine, not disrupt it.

Although technology is useful, it's a good idea to balance your use of digital and analog tools. Apps are convenient, but sometimes, a handwritten list or a physical calendar is better because it gives you tactile feedback that keeps you grounded. You want to harness the benefits of technology without becoming beholden to it, and if you can do this, you'll have a system that supports your routines and improves your efficiency and peace of mind.

Technology evolves rapidly, and so do your needs, so you want to reassess the effectiveness of your technological tools regularly to check that they still serve their intended purpose. Think about your recent experiences with the apps you use. Are certain features underutilized, or is there a recurring technical issue that causes you frustration? You might need to switch to a new app or update your settings so that they fit better with your current routine and the technology continues to be helpful to you.

With technology seamlessly woven into your routines, you'll be better equipped to tackle daily tasks confidently and efficiently, and this will give you space for personal growth—which is the next topic we'll explore.

11

SELF-REFLECTION AND PERSONAL GROWTH

Your path to organization isn't just about finding the right systems - it's about discovering who you are when you stop apologizing for how your mind works and start celebrating its unique brilliance.

Improving your organization is an ongoing journey. No matter how good you get at it, there will always be areas you can improve upon, and you'll need to be able to adjust as your circumstances change. We've talked a lot about self-reflection already, and this is going to be key to your ability to do this. Your organizational journey is a chapter of personal growth, and it's going to continue to evolve as you do. Let's look more closely at how you can make sure this happens.

IDENTIFYING YOUR STRENGTHS AND WEAKNESSES

Recognizing your strengths and weaknesses is the first step toward empowerment and growth. When you know what you excel at, your confidence naturally flourishes, and this means you can harness your strengths in ways you might not otherwise have considered. Conversely, understanding your weaknesses shows you where you need to improve, and this will mean you can focus your attention on the areas where it will have the most impact.

There are several things that can help you pinpoint your strengths and weaknesses. Self-assessments and feedback surveys are good if you'd like a more structured approach, and they can give you insights that might not be immediately apparent. If you'd prefer a more exploratory approach, introspective exercises, such as questionnaires, might be a better fit for you, guiding you to explore your thoughts and behaviors in a focused manner. They can show you patterns and preferences that you may not be aware of, and this, in turn, will tell where you thrive and the areas in which you might struggle. You can always ask your friends for input, too. An outside perspective on your capabilities might be just what you need to see the full picture.

Once you've identified your strengths, the next step is to use them to your advantage, particularly in organizing and decluttering. Doing this will make each task feel more achievable. For example, if you know you're good at creative problem-solving, you can use this ability to devise unique storage solutions that suit your lifestyle. If you're naturally detail-oriented, you can apply this skill to categorize items meticulously. It's when we focus on what we do best that we can navigate obstacles more effectively because we're approaching them from an angle that suits our skill sets.

Your weaknesses aren't things to feel bad about, although I know that inclination if you tend toward perfectionism. They're the things that you get to work on in order to grow as a person. Set realistic yet challenging and specific goals for skill development that will push you to expand your capabilities. Use the chapters in this book that target the areas you want to improve upon to equip yourself with new techniques and perspectives and celebrate each small victory as it comes along. Each step forward is a testament to your resilience and determination. When you can approach your weaknesses as opportunities for development, you'll shift your mindset from limitation to growth, and this will give you a more balanced and empowered sense of self.

Personal Strengths and Weaknesses Assessment

Take a moment to reflect on your strengths and weaknesses. Consider the following questions to guide your assessment:

- What activities or tasks make you feel energized and confident?
- What feedback have you received from others about your abilities?
- In which areas do you feel less confident or struggle to maintain focus?

Document your reflections and use them as a foundation for setting personal and professional goals.

JOURNALING FOR ADHD SELF-DISCOVERY

Hopefully, you've started the process of reflecting on your personal ADHD journey as you've been learning the skills and strategies in this book. If not, now's the time to start! For adults with ADHD, journaling can be extremely helpful. Writing allows you to untangle the threads of your experiences, and it helps you to understand the layers of emotions and thoughts that often jumble together. Clarity and focus are often challenging for people with ADHD, and journaling can help you with this. By putting pen to paper, you'll create a safe space to explore your inner world and express the whirlwind of emotions you feel. Then, you can examine them and begin to see patterns you may not otherwise notice, which will put you on a path toward healing and growth.

You might think that journaling has to look a certain way, but there are several approaches you can take. One approach is stream-of-consciousness writing, a process in which you allow your thoughts to flow freely onto the page without filtering or editing. This unfiltered exploration can tell you more about your subconscious thoughts and feelings, and it will give you an idea of what might be driving your behaviors and emotions. Another approach is to use guided prompts that provide structure for reflection. These are prompts you can come up with yourself, but you'll find a small starter kit at the end of this section. Prompts direct your writing and encourage you to pause and consider aspects of your life that you might otherwise let slip by unnoticed. Gratitude journaling is my favorite approach, though. It keeps me in a positive mindset because it makes me focus on the good things in my life, no matter how small they might be. When you acknowledge what you appreciate on a daily basis, you cultivate a habit of positivity, which can counterbalance the negative self-talk that often accompanies ADHD.

To really reap the benefits of journaling, though, you have to be consistent about it. It needs to be part of your routine rather than an occasional activity. Set aside a dedicated time each day or each week to write, and choose a comfortable, distraction-free environment where you can focus without being interrupted. Being consistent in both your timing and the location will help to reinforce the habit, and this will make it easier to maintain in the long term. Nonetheless, as with everything else we've talked about, flexibility is important. If one approach doesn't work, make adjustments until you find what feels right for you.

Writing down your thoughts and feelings is helpful, but it's when you reflect on your entries that you'll begin to see your growth and work on the areas you're still struggling with. As you review your past entries, look for recurring themes or patterns in your thoughts and behaviors. You might notice a repeated struggle with procrastination or a recurring feeling of overwhelm in certain situations, for example. If you can identify these patterns, you'll be able to address the underlying issues more effectively. Use your reflections to set intentions for your personal development. For example, if you recognize a pattern of stress related to time management, you might set an intention to explore time-blocking techniques or mindfulness practices to enhance your focus. What I love about journaling is that it builds self-awareness and empowers you to take steps toward growth, and I've found it so helpful on my own journey.

Journaling Prompts for Self-Discovery

Explore your thoughts and emotions with the following prompts:

- What is one lesson I learned today?
- How did I overcome a challenge this week?
- What am I grateful for right now?

Use these prompts as a starting point to deepen your self-awareness and uncover the layers of your experiences.

REFLECTION ACTIVITIES TO FOSTER GROWTH

Reflection allows us to understand the deeper lessons within our experiences. I think it's particularly helpful for those of us with ADHD because our minds are often racing with thoughts and emotions. Structured reflection can help with this and push us toward personal growth. It encourages us to pause, think critically, and evaluate our actions and decisions, and this is something I definitely need that structure for. When you dedicate time to reflection, you can gain insights into your behaviors, uncover patterns, and explore how your experiences shape your present and your future. You'll gain a deeper understanding of yourself, and this will make it easier for you to make informed decisions that align with your goals and values.

There are several reflection activities that can enhance your self-awareness and promote organizational self-improvement. A SWOT analysis, commonly used in business, can be adapted for personal development. This asks you to identify your **S**trengths, **W**eaknesses, **O**pportunities, and **T**hreats in order to get a comprehensive view of your current state, which will help you to strategize and plan effectively. Another activity that may help is a reflection walk, which is where you engage in mindful contemplation while walking. The rhythmic movement and natural surroundings can inspire clarity and creativity, and it will encourage your thoughts to surface naturally.

Incorporating reflection activities into your daily life doesn't require a complete overhaul of your routine. It's as easy as setting aside a few minutes each day, perhaps before bed, to reflect on your day. It can actually help you unwind, process events, and prepare for the next day with a clear mind. You can also use it at any point in your day as a decision-making tool. When you're faced with a choice, take a moment to consider your past experiences and the lessons they taught you, and allow these things to guide you. It can make a real difference to how you approach challenges, and it can make you more productive and less stressed out by the process of making a decision.

To get the most out of your reflection process, you'll need to evaluate its impact on your growth. Pay attention to changes in your behavior or mindset. Do you notice a shift in how you approach tasks or interact with others? Are you more patient, focused, or confident? These changes are indicators that your reflection is contributing to your growth. Ask your friends and family if they've noticed any difference, too. They may be able to see improvements that you can't see in yourself. Bear in mind, though, that reflection is an ongoing process, and its effects can be subtle. Don't expect to see massive changes right away. Just keep checking in to make sure your reflective practices are relevant and effective, and I'm sure you'll find that they support your growth.

EMBRACING CONTINUOUS IMPROVEMENT

Continuous improvement is the idea that we are always in a state of becoming, constantly growing, and learning. Adopting a commitment to lifelong learning will help you with this. You might choose to learn a new skill, refine an existing one, or embrace a new experience; each of these things will help you cultivate a mindset that values progress over perfection. You're doing this when you're organizing and decluttering, celebrating each small achievement, and recognizing that improvement is an ongoing process. If you keep doing this, you'll come to believe that every step, no matter how small, is contributing toward a larger goal, and this will allow you to move away from the idea of perfection and focus on continuous growth. Remember that failures are not setbacks; they're learning tools that offer insights into what doesn't work. When you embrace failure as part of the learning process, you can develop a more robust and flexible mindset, one that's open to change and innovation.

Your environment must also support continuous improvement if you're to be successful with this. Try to encourage a culture of feedback and collaboration, where open communication and shared experiences lead to collective growth. This doesn't have to be limited to your professional life; it could also be in your personal life or within a community. In fact, this is ideal. You want it in all areas of your life. Access resources that support ongoing education and development, whether through workshops, courses, or simply engaging with new information. Surround yourself with people who inspire and challenge you and who will provide constructive feedback and encourage you to push your boundaries. It's in these environments that you'll find the support and motivation you need to pursue your goals with confidence and determination.

Again, make sure you celebrate your progress. Reflect on the milestones you've reached and the achievements you've made, no matter how small they may seem. Recognize the hard work and dedication that got you there. Reward yourself for reaching each milestone, even if it's just through a simple acknowledgment. This will build a positive mindset, reinforce helpful behaviors, and motivate you to keep striving for excellence.

There's no destination with continuous improvement; it's all about the ongoing process of learning and growing. When you develop this mindset, you'll find that life is richer and more fulfilling, and for me, it also comes with greater self-acceptance. Embracing continuous improvement means accepting that you're always a work in progress and that each day offers new opportunities for growth and discovery. There's something very exciting about that.

12

LONG-TERM SUCCESS AND EMPOWERMENT

The path to lasting organization isn't a straight line - it's a spiral of growth, where each loop brings a deeper understanding of your remarkable mind. Today isn't the end of your journey; it's the beginning of your empowered future.

Continuous growth may be about the journey rather than the destination, but this doesn't mean that you can't keep your eye on long-term success. In fact, your growth is going to be key to it.

VIEWING ADHD AS A LIFELONG ASSET

You probably haven't thought much about ADHD being an asset before, but it brings you unique strengths, and if you can recognize this, you'll be able to reframe your perception of it. As we've seen, many adults with ADHD possess a creative spark that fuels innovative problem-solving. If this is true of you, it gives you the ability to see connections where others see none, to think outside the box, and to approach challenges from angles that other people overlook. You have a powerful tool that can lead to breakthroughs in whatever you're working on, and that's something to be celebrated. You might find that your mind naturally weaves together disparate ideas, crafting effective yet unconventional solutions. This kind of thinking can be a tremendous asset in fields that value innovation, such as technology, design, or entrepreneurship, and it's incredibly useful in your personal life, too.

As we've discussed, high energy and enthusiasm are other hallmark traits of ADHD that can be channeled into lifelong success. When you direct this energy toward your projects and passions, it can drive you to achieve remarkable feats.

To embrace a positive identity with ADHD, you'll need to recognize it as an integral part of who you are and value these strengths. Your identity is not defined by your limitations but by the potential for growth and achievement, and ADHD is a part of that. To reinforce your positive self-image, try sharing stories about your successes. Reflect on moments where your ADHD traits have led to accomplishments or unique insights. Perhaps it was a creative solution that saved a project or the boundless energy that helped you persevere through a demanding challenge. Each time you tell a story like this, you'll remind yourself of your capability and resilience. Reframing challenges as opportunities for growth will help you to do this, too. Remember that every obstacle is a chance to learn, adapt, and evolve, and no setback is ever a failure.

By making a conscious choice to view ADHD as an asset, you'll cultivate a mindset that celebrates your strengths and embraces the challenges as catalysts for growth. As you continue to explore and express these elements of your identity, remember that ADHD is a part of you— and it's a source of strength when you know how to use it to your advantage.

EMPOWERMENT THROUGH EDUCATION AND ADVOCACY

Empowerment begins with your own education. Staying informed about ADHD will improve your own understanding and also equip you to advocate effectively for both yourself and others. Read the latest research and literature so that you're up-to-date on new findings and strategies; this may help you with your organization and any other challenges you face. Engage in discussions, both online and offline, to dispel myths and stereotypes that often surround ADHD. When you share accurate information, you'll help to reduce the stigma around neurodiversity and contribute to a more informed community. If enough people do this, over time, we'll create an environment that's supportive, understanding, and better equipped to accommodate our specific needs.

When it comes to advocating for your personal needs, you need to be able to communicate effectively. Prepare for conversations with employers, educators, or family members to make sure that you can clearly articulate your needs and the accommodations that would help you thrive. Consider writing down your thoughts beforehand, outlining your challenges and your proposed solutions to them. You can then negotiate to reach a mutual agreement that will benefit both parties. Advocating for yourself isn't about demanding special treatment; it's about ensuring that you have the tools and support needed to stay organized and perform at your best. You might even find that, as you become more adept at advocacy, these skills will inspire you to advocate for other people within the ADHD community, too.

Reflection Time! Advocacy Role-Playing Scenario

Practice your advocacy skills with this role-playing scenario. Imagine a conversation with an employer about the accommodations that would benefit you in your workplace. Write down the key points you want to convey, focusing on clear communication and mutual understanding. This will build your confidence and prepare you to advocate for yourself when you need to.

CELEBRATING SUCCESS AND LOOKING FORWARD

I've said it before, and I'll say it again: Every milestone you reach, no matter how small, deserves recognition, and it will contribute to your success in the long term. Create rituals or traditions to mark your accomplishments and share these moments with friends and family to amplify the joy.

Celebrating your successes is important, but it's also important not to become complacent. Use them to spur you on to set future goals that are both inspiring and aligned with your personal values. Identify what truly matters to you, those long-term dreams that resonate deeply, and break them down into manageable steps. Your success is your motivation to keep going, but there should always be a new goal to chase.

To maintain a forward-thinking mindset, you'll need to be prepared to embrace the unknown and view change as an opportunity rather than a threat. I know it's not always easy to do this, but it will allow you to remain open to new experiences and learning, and that's how you're going to achieve personal growth. It's true that uncertainty can be daunting, but it also holds the potential for discovery and innovation. If you can adopt this mindset, you'll be in a great position to seize every opportunity that arises and adapt to curveballs with grace. What you'll find is that being open to change will improve your problem-solving abilities and enrich your life with diverse experiences and perspectives.

As you celebrate your successes and look toward the future, remember that the journey is ongoing. You're in a beautiful and continuous cycle of growth, reflection, and renewal, and this is the pathway to a fulfilling and empowered life.

KEEPING THE DREAM ALIVE: FROM CHAOS TO CALM

Wow - what a journey we've been on together! From drowning in clutter to discovering strategies that actually work for our wonderfully unique ADHD brains. Remember that feeling of finding your keys on the first try? Or walking into a room that stays organized for more than five minutes? Pretty amazing, right?

You now have tools to transform chaos into calm - real strategies that work with your brain instead of against it. But here's something even more exciting: you have the power to help others find their way too!

By sharing your experience on Amazon, you'll be like a friendly guide saying "Hey, I've been there too - and there's hope!" Your words could help another person with ADHD:

- Find peace in their space
- Stop feeling ashamed about their challenges
- Discover strategies that work for their unique brain
- Start their journey from overwhelm to confidence

The ADHD community grows stronger when we share our stories and support each other. Your review isn't just feedback - it's a beacon of hope for someone else who's searching for answers.

Ready to make a difference?

Thank you for being part of this supportive community. Together, we're showing that ADHD organization isn't about fitting into neurotypical boxes - it's about creating systems that celebrate how our minds work!

With gratitude and excitement for your continued journey!

CONCLUSION

Remember that Monday morning chaos we talked about in the beginning? That person who felt overwhelmed isn't gone - they've evolved into someone who understands that their different way of thinking isn't a flaw, but a gift waiting to be unleashed.

Your ADHD traits may sometimes present challenges, but they're also strengths that you can use to improve your organizational skills and promote personal growth. The decluttering hacks we've looked at here, along with a positive mindset, will give you everything you need to reshape your environment and, in turn, your life.

Remember the core messages we've discussed and try to build them into your daily life. There's no reason you can't bring organization to your life; you just may need to use strategies different from those of your neurotypical friends. Personalize your routines so that they suit your needs and bring you structure and peace. Use your skills to find the organizational techniques that work for you.

Now, it's time for you to take action! Here's my challenge to you: Do something to improve the organization in your home right now. Remember, you're going to start with small, manageable steps… and there's no time like the present to take the first one! Implement a five-minute pickup routine or start organizing your first drawer. Within the next half hour, you'll have a victory to celebrate, and this will build momentum and boost your confidence.

I want to remind you that you're capable of achieving your goals, and ADHD should never hold you back. Celebrate each step forward, no matter how small it is. After all, progress is progress, and every little bit counts. Embrace your creativity, energy, and enthusiasm, and never stop searching for opportunities to learn and grow.

I'm genuinely grateful for the opportunity to share this journey with you. Writing this book has been a victory of mine, and you can be sure I celebrated when I finished it. I'm grateful for the opportunity to share the things that have helped me, and I'm honored to be a part of your journey toward a more organized and fulfilling life.

As you move forward, carry with you the lessons and insights from this book. Approach each day with confidence in the fact that you have the tools to create a life that reflects your potential and aspirations. Remember, every step you take is a testament to your resilience and capability. Here's to a future filled with calm, focus, and the joy of embracing your authentic self. I'm rooting for you!

REFERENCES

Ackerman, C. E. (2023, June 10). *Cognitive restructuring techniques for reframing thoughts.* PositivePsychology.com. https://positivepsychology.com/cbt-cognitive-restructuring-cognitive-distortions/

Adams, J. (2017, December 7). *Put tiny tasks on your to-do list.* Peace of Mind Organizing | Professional Organizing in St. Louis, MO. https://www.peaceofmindorganizing.com/blog/put-tiny-tasks-on-your-to-do-list

Arnsten, A. (2010). The Emerging Neurobiology of Attention Deficit Hyperactivity Disorder: The Key Role of the Prefrontal Association Cortex. *J Pediatr, 54*(5).

Barkley, R. (2019, October 3). *What is executive function? 7 deficits tied to ADHD.* ADDitude. https://www.additudemag.com/7-executive-function-deficits-linked-to-adhd/

Barnes, D. (2015, April 27). *Hyperactive movements help ADHD children learn.* University of Mississippi Medical Center. https://www.umc.edu/news/News_Articles/2015/April/Researcher--Hyperactive-movements-help-ADHD-children-learn.html

Belsky, G. (2023, October 5). *What is executive function?* Understood. https://www.understood.org/en/articles/what-is-executive-function

Bennett, J. (2024, February 15). *15 soothing decor ideas to help you relax and unwind at home.* Better Homes & Gardens. https://www.bhg.com/decorating/lessons/basics/home-decorating-ideas-to-create-a-soothing-environment/

Bettino, K. (2021, May 24). *9 tips for creating a routine for adults with ADHD.* Psych Central. https://psychcentral.com/adhd/9-tips-for-creating-a-routine-for-adults-with-adhd

Bhandari, S. (2023, July 19). *What is emotional dysregulation?* WebMD. https://www.webmd.com/mental-health/what-is-emotional-dysregulation

Bozhilova, N. S., Michelini, G., Kuntsi, J., & Asherson, P. (2018). Mind wandering perspective on attention-deficit/hyperactivity disorder. *Neuroscience & Biobehavioral Reviews, 92,* 464–476. https://doi.org/10.1016/j.neubiorev.2018.07.010

Brice, R. (2023, October 23). *A User's Guide: I Have ADHD, So Why Am I So Exhausted?* Healthline. https://www.healthline.com/health/ADHD/adhd-fatigue

Bubl, E., Dörr, M., Riedel, A., Ebert, D., Philipsen, A., Bach, M., & Tebartz van Elst, L. (2015). Elevated background noise in adult attention deficit hyperactivity disorder is associated with inattention. *PLOS ONE, 10*(2), e0118271. https://doi.org/10.1371/journal.pone.0118271

Building Resilience: How Cognitive Flexibility and Emotional Regulation Empower ADHD Individuals. (2023, October 17). Effective Effort Consulting. https://effectiveeffortconsulting.com/building-resilience-how-cognitive-flexibility-and-emotional-regulation-empower-adhd-individuals/

Clear, J. (2018). *Atomic habits: An easy and proven way to build good habits and break bad ones.* Avery.

Cognitive therapy for attention deficit hyperactivity disorder. (n.d.). NYU Langone Health. https://nyulangone.org/conditions/attention-deficit-hyperactivity-disorder/treatments/cognitive-therapy-for-attention-deficit-hyperactivity-disorder

Corsini, C. (2024, June 27). *How to use affirmations to reprogram the subconscious mind.* Chris Corsini. https://chriscorsini.com/blogs/news/how-to-use-affirmations-to-reprogram-the-subconscious-mind

Craig, H. (2019, March 9). *Mindfulness at work: Create calm & focus in the workplace.* PositivePsychology.com. https://positivepsychology.com/mindfulness-at-work/

Cummins, M. (2019, December 31). *The 8 Tips ADHD Adults Need To Use To Avoid Stuck Thinking.* MarlaCummins. https://marlacummins.com/8-tips-adhd-adults-use-to-avoid-stuck-thinking/

Cummins, M. (2024, February 9). *ADHD & Finding Your Motivation When You're Not Interested.* Marla Cummins. https://marlacummins.com/adhd-finding-your-motivation-when-youre-not-interested/

Cussons, A. (2020, April 8). *S.W.O.T analysis for personal development.* Andrew Cussons - ActionCOACH. https://andrewcussons.actioncoach.co.uk/s-w-o-t-analysis-for-personal-development/

Dodson, W. (2020, February 28). *How ADHD ignites RSD: Meaning & medication solutions.* ADDitude. https://www.additudemag.com/rejection-sensitive-dysphoria-and-adhd/

Durand, G., Arbone, I., & Wharton, M. (2020). Reduced organizational skills in adults with ADHD are due to deficits in persistence, not in strategies. *PeerJ, 8*, e9844. https://doi.org/10.7717/peerj.9844

Enright, J. (2022, March 11). *How executive dysfunction impacts daily life.* LinkedIn. https://www.linkedin.com/pulse/how-executive-dysfunction-impacts-daily-life-jillian-enright

Famous people with ADHD. (2023, October 2). ADDitude. https://www.additudemag.com/slideshows/famous-people-with-adhd/

Fleming, S. (2023, October 2). *Should I do this or should I do that?: CBT for indecision.*

REFERENCES | 133

Beck Institute. https://beckinstitute.org/blog/should-i-do-this-or-should-i-do-that-cbt-for-indecision/

4 effective strategies for getting more done with ADHD. (2023, March 26). Sunsama. https://www.sunsama.com/blog/4-effective-strategies-for-getting-more-done-with-adhd

Genever, H. (2016, September 21). *4 colors that give you an unexpected productivity boost.* The Work Smarter Guide - Redbooth. https://redbooth.com/hub/colors-unexpected-productivity-boost/

Gillette, H. (2022, May 4). *ADHD freeze: Understanding task paralysis.* Psych Central. https://psychcentral.com/adhd/adhd-paralysis

Gillmore, C. (2023, November 14). *The psychology of space: How furniture impacts your well-being.* GILLMORE. https://www.gillmorespace.com/blog/post/the-psychology-of-space-how-furniture-impacts-your-well-being

Gordon, S. (2024, April 24). *The Connection Between Cleanliness and Mental Health.* Verywell Mind. https://www.verywellmind.com/how-mental-health-and-cleaning-are-connected-5097496

Gotter, A. (2023, March 22). *8 Breathing Exercises to Try When You Feel Anxious.* Healthline. https://www.healthline.com/health/breathing-exercises-for-anxiety

Green, R. (2023, May 11). *Time blindness in ADHD.* Verywell Mind. https://www.verywellmind.com/causes-and-symptoms-of-time-blindness-in-adhd-5216523

Groenewegen, C. (2024, February 19). *How to use the 2-Minute rule for more productivity and less procrastination.* AI Project and Task Management | Plan Your Work Automatically (Try for Free). https://www.usemotion.com/blog/2-minute-rule

Heerema, E. (2015, August 29). *Using the Method of Loci for Memorization.* Verywell Health. https://www.verywellhealth.com/will-the-method-of-loci-mnemonic-improve-your-memory-98411

Hoshaw, C. (2022, March 29). *What is Mindfulness? A Simple Practice for Greater Well-being.* Healthline. https://www.healthline.com/health/mind-body/what-is-mindfulness

Houlton, L. (2024, April 29). *How to create an ADHD-friendly home – for a more productive, relaxing space.* homesandgardens.com. https://www.homesandgardens.com/solved/how-to-create-an-adhd-friendly-home

How Can Technology and Apps Be Leveraged to Enhance Productivity and Organization for Adults with ADHD? (n.d.). Envision ADHD. https://www.envisionadhd.com/single-post/how-can-technology-and-apps-be-leveraged-to-enhance-productivity-and-organization-for-adults-with-ad

How Simone biles turned ADHD into her superpower. (2024, August 6). LDRFA. https://www.ldrfa.org/simone-biles-turned-adhd-into-her-superpower/

How to foster a growth mindset in the classroom. (2020, December 10). School of

134 | REFERENCES

Education Online. https://soeonline.american.edu/blog/growth-mindset-in-the-classroom/

Iyer, K. (2023, August 28). *Differences between intrinsic and extrinsic rewards.* HubEngage. https://www.hubengage.com/employee-recognition/exploring-the-differences-between-intrinsic-and-extrinsic-rewards/

Jaffe, E. (2015, February 18). *How Impulsiveness Can Boost Your Creativity.* fastcompany.com. https://www.fastcompany.com/3042505/how-impulsiveness-can-boost-your-creativity

Jarrett, C. (2020, May 14). *Why procrastination is about managing emotions, not time.* BBC. https://www.bbc.co.uk/worklife/article/20200121-why-procrastination-is-about-managing-emotions-not-time

Kedia, G. (2023, September 18). *Procrastination, fear of failure, and perfectionism.* A Brilliant Mind. https://abrilliantmind.blog/why-do-we-procrastinate-part-3-fear-of-failure/

Kolberg, J. (2024, October 14). *33 ADHD-friendly ways to get organized.* ADDitude. https://www.additudemag.com/how-to-get-organized-with-adhd/

Laub, E. (2024, June 24). *ADHD Paralysis: Why It Happens & How to Overcome It.* Choosing Therapy. https://www.choosingtherapy.com/adhd-paralysis/

Lebow, H. I. (2021, June 24). *How to Stay Productive with ADHD.* Psych Central. https://psychcentral.com/adhd/adhd-productivity-strategies-for-getting-things-done

Lebson, C. (2024, July 8). *My ADHD journey: Thriving through variety.* LinkedIn. https://www.linkedin.com/pulse/my-adhd-journey-thriving-through-variety-cory-lebson-qosje

Leonard, K., & Watts, R. (2024, July 9). *The ultimate guide to S.M.A.R.T. Goals.* Forbes Advisor. https://www.forbes.com/advisor/business/smart-goals/

Liao, S. (2024, July 4). *How to Use Hyperfocus for Good.* WebMD. https://www.webmd.com/add-adhd/ss/slideshow-adhd-hyperfocus-tips

Lomas, E. (2023, December 4). *14 science-backed ways to wind down before bed.* The Pulse Blog. https://ouraring.com/blog/tips-to-wind-down-before-bed/

Mahindru, A., Patil, P., & Agrawal, V. (2023). Role of physical activity on mental health and well-being: A review. *Cureus, 15*(1). https://doi.org/10.7759/cureus.33475

Martin, L., Oepen, R., Bauer, K., Nottensteiner, A., Mergheim, K., Gruber, H., & Koch, S. (2018). Creative arts interventions for stress management and prevention—A systematic review. *Behavioral Sciences, 8*(2), 28. https://doi.org/10.3390/bs8020028

Martins, J. (2024, February 25). *Are you time blocking your calendar? Here's why you should start now.* Asana. https://asana.com/resources/what-is-time-blocking

Miller, L. (2021, June 15). *What is cognitive flexibility, and why does it matter?* BetterUp. https://www.betterup.com/blog/cognitive-flexibility

Moore, W. (2024, May 25). *How to build habits with ADHD.* Level up In Life with MooreMomentum. https://mooremomentum.com/blog/how-to-build-habits-with-adhd/

Neff. (2024, August 20). *How to deal with rejection sensitive dysphoria.* Insights of a Neurodivergent Clinician. https://neurodivergentinsights.com/blog/how-to-deal-with-rejection-sensitive-dysphoria

Neff. (2024, June 23). *How the interest-based nervous system drives ADHD motivation.* Insights of a Neurodivergent Clinician. https://neurodivergentinsights.com/blog/adhd-motivation

Nicholson, B. (2024, February 5). *Your own worst enemy: Silencing negative self talk.* ADDitude. https://www.additudemag.com/slideshows/negative-self-talk-the-self-esteem-killers-you-control/

Oscar Berman, M., Blum, K., Chen, T. J., Braverman, E., Waite, R., Downs, W., Arcuri, V., Notaro, A., Palomo, T., & Comings. (2008). Attention-deficit-hyperactivity disorder and reward deficiency syndrome. *Neuropsychiatric Disease and Treatment, 4*(5), 893–918. https://doi.org/10.2147/ndt.s2627

Pacheco, D., & Rosen, D. (2023, December 5). *Bedtime Routines for Adults.* Sleep Foundation. https://www.sleepfoundation.org/sleep-hygiene/bedtime-routine-for-adults

Parker, H. (2024, November 22). *10 best ADHD productivity apps & tools for time management.* ClickUp. https://clickup.com/blog/adhd-productivity-tools/

Pedersen, T. (2023, October 17). *How Can Journaling Benefit Adults with ADHD?* Healthline. https://www.healthline.com/health/adhd/journaling-for-adhd

Pierce, R. (2023, March 17). *10-Minute tips to improve flexible thinking.* Life Skills Advocate. https://lifeskillsadvocate.com/blog/10-minute-tips-to-improve-flexible-thinking/

Porter, E. (2023, April 10). *ADHD and Hyperfocus.* Healthline. https://www.healthline.com/health/adhd/adhd-symptoms-hyperfocus

The power of ergonomic furniture for Neurodivergent individuals. (2023, June 14). Home office Space NZ. https://www.homeofficespace.co.nz/blogs/home-office-blog/enhancing-focus-and-productivity-the-power-of-ergonomic-furniture-for-neurodivergent-individuals?

Priority matrix: How to identify what matters and get more done. (2024, January 20). Asana. https://asana.com/resources/priority-matrix

Racasan, R. (2023, November 28). *These are the 6 best candle scents for sleep, say experts - 'they're a natural aid to help you drift away!'.* livingetc.com. https://www.livingetc.com/advice/candle-scents-for-sleep

Ramsay, R. (2024, August 21). *ADHD and anxiety: Symptoms, connections & coping mechanisms*. ADDitude. https://www.additudemag.com/adhd-and-anxiety-symptoms-coping/

Raypole, C. (2021, October 7). *How Can CBT Help with ADHD Symptoms?* Healthline. https://www.healthline.com/health/adhd/cbt-for-adhd

Rejection sensitive dysphoria: 10 signs you might have RSD and 5 ways to manage it. (2024, February 14). Newport Institute. https://www.newportinstitute.com/resources/mental-health/rejection-sensitive-dysphoria/

Richard, V., Lebeau, J., Becker, F., Inglis, E. R., & Tenenbaum, G. (2018). Do more creative people adapt better? An investigation into the association between creativity and adaptation. *Psychology of Sport and Exercise, 38*, 80-89. https://doi.org/10.1016/j.psychsport.2018.06.001

Ro, C. (2023, July 21). *Can houseplants purify the air in your home?* BBC News. https://www.bbc.co.uk/news/business-66186492

Roggli, L. (2024, February 20). *How to Declutter with an ADHD brain: Organization solutions for real life.* ADDitude. https://www.additudemag.com/slideshows/how-to-declutter-adhd/

Rollins, K. (2020, January 28). *Memory tricks: ADHDer see, ADHDer do.* ADDitude. https://www.additudemag.com/memory-tricks-adhder-see-adhder-do/

Roselló, B., Berenguer, C., Baixauli, I., Mira, Á., Martinez-Raga, J., & Miranda, A. (2020). Empirical examination of executive functioning, ADHD associated behaviors, and functional impairments in adults with persistent ADHD, remittent ADHD, and without ADHD. *BMC Psychiatry, 20*(1). https://doi.org/10.1186/s12888-020-02542-y

Russell, M. (2024, May 30). *Why celebrating small wins matters.* Harvard Summer School. https://summer.harvard.edu/blog/why-celebrating-small-wins-matters/

Saline, S. (2022, March 22). *Hyperfocus and ADHD: Productivity superpower or Kryptonite?* Psychology Today. https://www.psychologytoday.com/us/blog/your-way-adhd/202203/hyperfocus-and-adhd-productivity-superpower-or-kryptonite

Sanilevici, M., Reuveni, O., Lev-Ari, S., Golland, Y., & Levit-Binnun, N. (2021). Mindfulness-based stress reduction increases mental wellbeing and emotion regulation during the first wave of the COVID-19 pandemic: A synchronous online intervention study. *Frontiers in Psychology, 12.* https://doi.org/10.3389/fpsyg.2021.720965

Schuman-Olivier, Z., Trombka, M., Lovas, D. A., Brewer, J. A., Vago, D. R., Gawande, R., Dunne, J. P., Lazar, S. W., Loucks, E. B., & Fulwiler, C. (2020). Mindfulness and Behavior Change. *Harv Rev Psychiatry, 28*(6), 371–394. https://doi.org/10.1097/HRP.0000000000000277

Scott, E. (2024, February 12). *What Is Body Scan Meditation?* Verywell Mind. https://www.verywellmind.com/body-scan-meditation-why-and-how-3144782

Shaw, P., Stringaris, A., Nigg, J., & Leibenluft, E. (2014). Emotional dysregulation and Attention-Deficit/Hyperactivity Disorder. *Am J Psychiatry, 171*(3), 276–293. https://doi.org/10.1176/appi.ajp.2013.13070966

Shedding light on eye strain: 10 expert tips to perfect your Home Office lighting. (2023, March 29). BenQ Knowledge Centre. https://www.benq.eu/en-uk/knowledge-center/knowledge/shedding-light-on-eye-strain--10-expert-tips-to-perfect-your-hom.html

Sheldon, R., & Wigmore, I. (2022, September 15). *What is Pomodoro technique time management?* WhatIs.com. https://www.techtarget.com/whatis/definition/pomodoro-technique

Sherrell, Z. (2021, July 21). *6 strengths and benefits of ADHD.* Medical and health information. https://www.medicalnewstoday.com/articles/adhd-benefits

Sophia K. (2023, January 28). *An ADHD-friendly way to make a cleaning routine that works for you.* Neurodiverging. https://www.neurodiverging.com/an-adhd-friendly-way-to-make-a-cleaning-routine-that-works-for-you/

Steirer, A. (2023, November 3). *Branch out: 5 solid reasons to separate work and home spaces.* Greenleaf Workspace. https://www.greenleafworkspace.com/blogs/grow-learn-work-succeed/branch-out-5-solid-reasons-to-separate-work-and-home-spaces

Stillman, J. (2016, October 3). *This Foolproof 5-Minute Exercise Will Cure Your Procrastination.* Inc.com. https://www.inc.com/jessica-stillman/this-foolproof-5-minute-exercise-will-cure-your-procrastination.html

Thorson, M. (2023, February 9). *Hear me out: Walking can help us get to know ourselves better.* Well+Good. https://www.wellandgood.com/walking-self-reflection/

Townsend, K. (2021, September 13). *Goals, stretch goals and aspirations: What's the difference?* Kimberly Townsend. https://drkimberlytownsend.com/goals-stretch-goals-aspirations/

Tuckman, A. (2024, May 22). *ADHD minds are trapped in now (& other time management truths).* ADDitude. https://www.additudemag.com/time-management-skills-adhd-brain/

Turner, L. (2023, December 29). *ADHD-Friendly Home Office Design for Focus and Success.* autonomous. https://www.autonomous.ai/ourblog/adhd-friendly-home-office-design-for-focus

Urminsky, N. (2023, April 4). *The ADHD kitchen - Why layout matters.* Keeping Chaos Beautiful. https://www.keepingchaosbeautiful.com/post/the-adhd-kitchen-why-layout-matters

VanDerBill, B. (2022, January 6). *5 Surfaces You Need to Clean Off Now to Be More*

Productive. HerMoney. https://hermoney.com/enjoy/wellness/5-surfaces-you-need-to-clean-off-to-be-more-productive/

Vevers, S. (2024, January 15). *What to know about ADHD stimming.* MedicalNewsToday. https://www.medicalnewstoday.com/articles/adhd-stimming

Viering, T., Naaijen, J., Van Rooij, D., Thiel, C., Philipsen, A., Dietrich, A., Franke, B., Buitelaar, J., & Hoekstra, P. J. (2021). Amygdala reactivity and ventromedial prefrontal cortex coupling in the processing of emotional face stimuli in attention-deficit/hyperactivity disorder. *European Child & Adolescent Psychiatry, 31*(12), 1895-1907. https://doi.org/10.1007/s00787-021-01809-3

Whelan, C. (2021, May 6). *How to Manage Procrastination if You Have ADHD.* Healthline. https://www.healthline.com/health/adhd/adhd-procrastination

White, H. (2019, March 5). *The creativity of ADHD.* Scientific American. https://www.scientificamerican.com/article/the-creativity-of-adhd/

Yassin, F. (2023, September 13). *ADHD superpowers: Hyperfocus, creativity, and intuition.* thewaveclinic.com. https://thewaveclinic.com/blog/adhd-superpowers-hyperfocus-creativity-intuition/

Zylowska, L. (2024, June 11). *Meditation for the bored & restless: How to practice mindfulness with ADHD.* ADDitude. https://www.additudemag.com/how-to-practice-mindfulness-adhd/

Printed in Great Britain
by Amazon